LIFE GETS BETTER

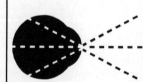

This Large Print Book carries the
Seal of Approval of N.A.V.H.

LIFE GETS BETTER

THE UNEXPECTED PLEASURES OF GROWING OLDER

WENDY LUSTBADER

THORNDIKE PRESS
A part of Gale, Cengage Learning

GALE
CENGAGE Learning®

Detroit • New York • San Francisco • New Haven, Conn • Waterville, Maine • London

GALE
CENGAGE Learning®

Copyright © 2011 by Wendy Lustbader.
Thorndike Press, a part of Gale, Cengage Learning.

Thorndike Press® Large Print Health, Home & Learning.
The text of this Large Print edition is unabridged.
Other aspects of the book may vary from the original edition.
Set in 16 pt. Plantin.

LIBRARY OF CONGRESS CATALOGING-IN-PUBLICATION DATA

Lustbader, Wendy.
  Life gets better : the unexpected pleasures of growing older / by Wendy Lustbader. — Large print ed.
    p. cm. — (Thorndike Press large print health, home & learning)
  Originally published: New York : J.P. Tarcher/Penguin, 2011.
  Includes bibliographical references.
  ISBN-13: 978-1-4104-4739-5 (hardcover)
  ISBN-10: 1-4104-4739-1 (hardcover)
  1. Self-confidence. 2. Self-actualization (Psychology) 3. Older people. 4. Large type books. I. Title.
BF575.S39L87 2012
155.67—dc23   2011051249

Published in 2012 by arrangement with Jerry P. Tarcher, a member of Penguin Group (USA), Inc.

Printed in the United States of America
1 2 3 4 5 6 7 16 15 14 13 12

In memory of my mother and father

MARJORIE HERSCH, 1930–2002
IRWIN LUSTBADER, 1927–2002

CONTENTS

ACKNOWLEDGMENTS

Writers need places to go where they can roost undisturbed. The Whiteley Center, a refuge of beauty and silence administered by the University of Washington, gave me a period of concentrated work on the book unlike any other. Kathy Cowell was an enthusiastic and thoughtful host. The Antique Sandwich Company allowed me to take up the table in the far back for hours on end, and I was always cheered by the welcome I received from the proprietor, Shirley Herridge. The Continental Restaurant has let me occupy the back corner table for thirty years and five books. Owner Helen Lagos has been unfailing in her warmth.

This book would not exist without the elders who told me their stories and who participated in our Tuesday afternoon discussions, one at Elderwise and the other at Heritage House. Trenchant remarks, deep observations, provocative exchanges — all of this enriched my understanding of later life, week after week. One participant, Tom Kugiya, died before I could tell him I included one of his tales in the book. He would have been delighted, and I name him here to honor him. Each one of the elders made an imprint on the text, either by voicing insights or helping me sustain my spirit for the project.

My agent, Jane Dystel, believed in the book from the first mention of the idea and urged me to bring it to fruition. I appreciate her vision and her sense of what the audience for this book would most value. My editors at Tarcher, Gabrielle Moss and Mitch Horowitz, were passionate in their encouragement all the way through. Their grasp of the book's themes, from the obvious to the subtle, gave me the impetus to keep peeling back the layers.

My gratitude goes especially to my manuscript readers who scouted out confusing paragraphs, repetitions, and sentences in need of renovation: JoAnn Damron-Rodriguez, Rich Goldman, Lauren Grosskopf, Linda Hermans, Chaz Hill, Irene Hull, Kathleen Sullivan, Valerie Trueblood, Jeff Welker, and Carter Catlett Williams. They saved me from embarrassment and challenged me to clarify my thinking, all while giving me fresh heart for the revisions they inspired.

My husband, Barry Grosskopf, read the manuscript twice with great care. His edits were characteristically sensitive, persistent, and accurate. Above all, I thank him for enduring my disappearances with loving support for what writers must do.

INTRODUCTION

"Don't worry," I called out to a bus full of world travelers, all between the ages of eighteen and twenty-four. "These are the worst years of your lives." Relief spread across the rows of faces at this stark and unexpected pronouncement. We were on a Kiwi Experience bus excursion, exploring North Island, New Zealand, and our driver had asked each of us to step up to his tour microphone and say a few words to break up the monotony of the sheep-filled landscape. My husband and I could have been the parents of everyone else on the bus, including the driver. "Everything gets better — you just have to get through your twenties," I emphasized, urging them to be patient with these years of struggle.

At the next rest stop, I was swarmed by the thankful. One tall, skinny fellow from Holland told me, "I don't know how to love, who to love, if I am gay or straight. I've been torturing myself over it — on and off, thinking of killing myself. Lady, you've given me hope." A 19-year-old blonde from England said she had been utterly depressed since leaving home for this journey, and that my remarks were like being shaken awake. She realized it would take time to arrive at the answers to the questions that were nagging at her. One person after another declared gratitude, each marveling at having never heard anyone say this before. Praise of youth had been pushed at them constantly, from all directions. "If this is really the best," said a 20-year-old from Denmark, "I don't even want the rest of it."

I saw the need for this book in the vehemence of the thanks I received that day. The myth of youth as the best time of life burdens the young and makes us all dread getting older, as though there is only diminishment of life's bounty as the decades pass. I realized a book would be welcomed that proclaims the opposite: Life gets better as we get older, on all levels except the physical.

Ten years have passed. I have been gathering my own life experiences and that of friends already a few decades into the richness of being elders. As a social worker, I have been listening to older people's stories for almost thirty years, hearing them attest to later life as the source of ever-expanding inner and outer discovery. Now in my mid-fifties, I see that my personal and professional lives have combined to give me a broad vantage point. This book merges my personal testimony with a vivid sampling of elders' voices garnered from diverse sources — interviews, therapy sessions, conversations with older friends, research articles, films, blogs, books, radio vignettes, and chance encounters on buses and in cafés.

Life Gets Better is a counterbalance to the negative and stultifying stereotypes about aging that constrain everyone's spirit. Using elders' personal accounts, I show the worship of youth to have been a colossal error. I depict the ways we grow in self-knowledge as we get older, how we derive valuable insight from our mistakes and misadventures, and how we gain confidence with each difficulty we surmount. The book is adorned with colorful portraits of the inner freedoms that come with getting older, especially those that stem from feeling less constrained by other people's judgments and expectations.

People in their twenties and thirties may particularly value this chance to satisfy their curiosity about what it is like to grow old.

Later life can seem to them like another universe entirely, and thus they want to know what really goes on. Having seen at least a few radiant older people, they hope to become privy to the secrets of aging well and a life well lived. Those who are struggling with questions of identity and meaning will grab hold of what older people have discovered in their own quest to construct good lives.

People in their forties and fifties want to feel the animation of viewing midlife as part of a grand progression, rather than a sorrowful dwindling. Having already tasted new liberties in leaving their youth behind, they crave the chance to have these gains defined and clearly articulated. The elders depicted here affirm for middle-aged and older people that the personal flourishing they have experienced actually comes with getting older and thus can be sustained.

It is time for all of us to discard our negative assumptions about aging, individually and collectively. Too often, we see that *old lady* over there, rather than a woman who has gotten older. When it comes to ourselves, we feel both distinctive and ageless inside. We each want to be seen as an individual, rather than one of *them*. We find it offensive to be thrust into a category called *the elderly,* simply on the basis of how long we have been alive. This book is full of whimsy and idiosyncrasy, the myriad ways we come into our own, as well as the universal truths that unite us across the lifespan.

A woman responded with enthusiasm to an article about the emotional benefits of getting older:

> At age fifty-six, my body has more aches and pains, but I love the way my brain is working. I make decisions more quickly, enjoy mental challenges, and come up with good solutions to problems without all the stress of my younger years. With each passing year I get happier.[1]

Researchers who examined a telephone survey of over 340,000 Americans in 2008 found that older people, on average, are "happier and less stressed" than younger people. They were surprised to find that variables such as "gender, having children under the age of eighteen at home, being unemployed, and not having a partner" had little impact on this tendency to feel happier with age.[2]

Later life is largely our own creation. While we exert less influence over the course of our early years, we must each decide what we want to make of our old age. A 62-year-old man said he had never considered the possibility that his life might actually be getting better as he got older. "I've only ever harped on the physical nuisances. The idea itself makes me want to take another look."

The elders quoted here have not avoided the hard questions or the many kinds of sadness, but searched out what might be transcendent. The resulting book is nonlinear. It advances for a while and then doubles back, exploring layers of understanding. Themes begun in earlier chapters reappear in other forms near the end, much as they do in life. No solutions are offered, since the process of aging is not posed as a problem but rather as a burgeoning opportunity.

■ ■ ■ ■

PART ONE:
HOPE

■ ■ ■ ■

1
SELF-KNOWLEDGE

The last of life, for which the first was
made

ROBERT BROWNING

"I know who I am," declares a character played by Olympia Dukakis in the film *Moonstruck.* It is one of those consummate moments in the movies when a great deal about life gets encapsulated in a sentence. She has been urged to do something that goes against her character, something that would benefit her materially but would violate a core principle by which she has lived her long life. She makes this declaration with the exuberance of certainty decades in the making.

As we get older, we become more and more ourselves. Assuming something about an 80-year-old person's capacities, based on age alone, is likely to be wrong, while we can usually generalize about an 8-year-old child's stage of development. Growing into our individuality is an accurate way to envision aging itself. It is no wonder, then, that our craving for freedom usually becomes intense by midlife. An increasingly vivid sense of self insists on release. When we think that exploration is only the province of youth, we impose a false constriction. There is actually more to be found once we know which aspects of life are within our reach and are worth seeking.

Shortly after my fiftieth birthday, I started attending a yoga class for beginners. Almost everyone in the room got right into the various postures and positions. I could not do a single one of them correctly. My knees refused to bend enough, my neck could only turn so far, my arms ached with the slightest stretch, and my face was quickly hot with embarrassment. This inflexibility was not related to aging; it was skeletal. In gym class in junior high, three physical education teachers once tried to hoist my back up off the mat into a bridge, to no avail. These many years later, the challenge was not to try to force unwilling joints to do the impossible, but to accept the body I was born with and do whatever I could with it.

Let it go. I issued this command to myself

with some vehemence. There was simply no point in feeling humiliated by something over which I had no control. I decided to flaunt my incapacity. I stood up in the middle of the lesson, walked over to the pile of supports and pillows in the corner, and dragged over a host of ways to prop up my errant torso and limbs. "Good," called out the teacher. "Everyone should make sure they are comfortable." Three or four other people went over and got what they needed. A few weeks later, one woman came up to me before class to thank me: "Without you always doing so much worse than me, I could never have stuck with it."

We are all good at something. I am not good at yoga. It was a relief to smile at my ineptitude, rather than condemn my body as inferior to the more flexible ones around me. Ever since that scene with the gym teachers, I had considered my body something of a freakish hulk with an unbending infrastructure. There in that yoga class, I let it be — at long last.

Self-acceptance is one of those life projects that can require a long struggle. Most of us are quick to see ourselves as deficient in comparison with others. These negative self-evaluations are then dragged along, weighing down our spirits unnecessarily for years.

Later life becomes the time to set ourselves free. One diminutive woman in her eighties told me, proudly, "These days, I really speak my mind." For most of her life, she had remained quiet, adapting to other people's needs and suppressing her own preferences. She had grown up as the fourth of eight children, with three outspoken older brothers, and married a man similar to them in his garrulous charm. A few years after his death, she explained her growing assertiveness: "Why not? What do I have to lose?" Her confidence was captivating. She was ready to be herself at long last.

Becoming oneself is a lifelong quest. Some younger people seem self-possessed, but this is not the same thing as the confidence that comes with getting older. Self-confidence that is earned over the years, rather than simply claimed, is much more resistant to external assaults. There is no substitute for having been tested by prior ordeals and having come out the other side more solid than before. Each time we stand our ground, each time we throw off comparison and envy, another layer of certainty is added to our view of ourselves.

Now I do Balkan folk dancing with my husband and about thirty other people. We link arms in a long, snaking line and move in unison to the music. Sometimes I cannot get the steps right when trying to learn a new dance. Then the whispers return. *Clumsy. Klutz.* Fortunately, I am able to silence my doubt, forego the effort to master the steps, and just feel the music. I keep in sync with the soothing motion of the line, letting the joy of it overtake me, and somehow my feet find the right way to move.

Our weaknesses may be hard to embrace, but we need to know them well if we do not want to be ruled by them. Our most maddening flaws, the ones we do not want to see and that make us wince when others try to show them to us, almost always have their origin in childhood. By the time we are fifty, we are lucky if we have attained a thorough grasp of these vulnerabilities. Most people only begin reaching inward in this manner in their fifth or sixth decade, having finally attained enough self-respect to face their most perplexing behaviors and emotions.

A partner experiences our flaws more vividly than anyone else. The ways we repeatedly hurt the person closest to us tend to be the key areas we need to examine. For this reason, finding a life partner and sticking with that person is one of the best means of attaining self-knowledge. Good fortune is having a partner who lets us know these things in a sympathetic way, but usually this information about ourselves reaches us in the form of reprisal and accusation. Each partner's own ancient reactivity gets mixed up in anger at the other's weaknesses, and thus it can become a messy enterprise.

Finding fault with a partner is considerably simpler than looking within. Most of us can supply a detailed account of the ways a partner has hurt or disappointed us, but we have only a skimpy recall of the ways we ourselves caused hurt and disappointment. Couples frequently retreat into a status quo that looks peaceful on the surface, while inwardly there is a kind of deadening disengagement. Too commonly, having an affair then becomes the route people use in order to feel alive again — sexually, emotionally, creatively.

Rather than leave, we would do better to shout our discontent from the rafters and start the dialogue that launches change. One 48-year-old man decided against an affair and instead demanded reconnection with a vivaciousness that was once the core of his marriage. He was delighted to find that his wife was ready and willing. They entered into a mutually courageous process of facing strains and conflicts they had avoided.

Shaking things up, rather than leaving, brought them both a welcome momentum toward a better life. Ten years later, they are both still changing in ways neither had suspected was possible for them as individuals or as a couple.

A certain degree of humility is necessary in order to learn as much as we can about troubling aspects of ourselves. Arrogant people tend to be the most insecure, having been too afraid to confront their limitations. Paradoxically, daring to examine criticisms for what truths they contain can lead to a deep-seated, unshakable kind of confidence. As we gain awareness of our interior geography, we acquire greater freedom of outward expression and can seek closeness to others without fearing what might be exposed.

"Color in one-third of the circle," commanded my third-grade teacher as I stood at the blackboard. She was trying to teach me fractions by fiat because I had missed a whole math section while out sick. I tried, but I could not for the life of me understand what I was supposed to do. The whole class laughed, and thus went my conception of myself. From then on, I harbored the secret that I was stupid.

As a psychotherapist, I frequently ask

people if they have any painful ideas about themselves carried from the past. I hear story after story of self-doubt, usually derived from thoughtless remarks made long ago by teachers, parents, or peers. The power of a single sentence to put a shroud over someone's life is greater than is generally recognized. Throughout high school and college, I believed that I did not deserve the straight A's I was getting. Only when I was elected to Phi Beta Kappa upon graduation did my secret finally lose its hold on me. When I help people identify false beliefs, usually encoded in one or two harsh sentences, I can sometimes see the shroud lift immediately.

Discovering our strengths also takes time. Everyone has individual gifts, and we have to give ourselves room to try out different skills. We need to persevere through the awkward initial phases of learning. At the outset of any undertaking, there are always plenty of people who seem miles beyond what we could ever achieve. Self-defeating ideas can easily take hold during the vulnerable phase when we are acquiring basic skills: *I'll never be able to do that.* It can seem as though others have it made, that they produce top-notch work almost effortlessly, when in reality a great deal of hard labor has led up to their apparent ease. Many people give up, convinced that they could never be as good as those they admire.

One way or another, we are often forced to find our way before we have had the time to explore our inclinations. Financial pressures often push us toward that which is most lucrative rather than most satisfying. We can also be misdirected into areas of endeavor that are not the best for us by excessive prodding from those who think they see our destiny more clearly than we do. In this regard, misplaced praise can be as dangerous to self-knowledge as derogatory remarks. It is best to sort through the compliments we get from others, to see what fits our inner sense, but in youth we can become trapped by heeding other people's hopes or trying to vanquish their anxieties.

In an art class I took in college, there was one person who stood out. He planted himself in the painting studio and worked away at canvases for days on end. The rest of us completed the paintings required to get credit for the class, but he challenged himself to develop his abilities far beyond this level. He was always there when I went to the studio to work on one of my paintings, no matter what time of day or night.

During one of the rare interludes when he would put down his paintbrush and talk, I learned that he came from a well-to-do family with great expectations for him to succeed either in business or one of the prestigious professions. For him, doing art came from a deep inner conviction, yet it was difficult to maintain his dedication while his family bore down on him with their disrespect for his chosen path. Ironically, their almost constant assault forced him to muster the kind of self-belief necessary to become a professional artist able to live off his work.

Many of us are not able to follow our heart's desire to this degree so early in life. In the first quadrant of adulthood, we may succumb to the positive verdict of success in one field, even though it is not the one for which we have been yearning. Then, long into midlife, it may be tempting to go on gathering accolades in ways that have come easily to us. That which kindles our fullest enthusiasm, however, might be located in another direction entirely, and it is in later life that we may finally let ourselves explore these dormant abilities and pursuits.

Most of us end up having to live through several possible solutions to the puzzle, *Who am I?* We may have to shed false ideas that we picked up from early hurts. It may be necessary to try out many variations of our interests and identities, casting off the linear progression that we followed for the sake of practicality. Often, we need to allow ourselves to move through a period of tentative groping for what feels right. In retrospect, we may recognize the answer. We find out who we love by loving, what we can do by trying things out, and what we need by aching from what remains unfulfilled.

Cheryl Richey had been a university professor for thirty years when she retired from her tenured position and became an artist. She had taken an art class about four years earlier and could not shed the memory of the excitement that had gripped her during the class. Her academic career had been satisfying on many levels, but making art seemed to call forth parts of her that had been awaiting release. For a while, she worked on paintings while teaching part-time, until she finally got up the courage to show her portfolio to colleagues. "I can remember feeling so vulnerable, shy, and nervous about it because it was a hidden and private part of myself. But uniformly, the reactions were extremely positive." She has gone on to paint full-time and to exhibit her work at numerous juried shows and galleries.[1]

So much of youth is consumed by trying to figure out what we are good at, which skills to develop, and which to set aside. Our early views of ourselves are often too limiting, sometimes excluding heartfelt passions or proving to be entirely at odds with who we later turn out to be. Getting older often brings relief from the need to comply with external dictates. Instead of remaining encased in prior judgments about what we can and cannot do, we realize it is time to let our individual story unfold. At last, we may garner sufficient confidence to say, *This is who I am.*

2
GRATITUDE

It is not happiness that makes us grateful,
but gratefulness that makes us happy.
BROTHER DAVID STEINDL-RAST

In youth, we often feel cheated when things
do not go our way. Our expectations are
tinged with a sense of entitlement, as
though life owes us certain benefits. When
mishaps impede us, we begrudge them, as
though we should have been exempt. Then
in our middle years, we become lulled by
daily routines and commitments. We take
our relationships for granted and barely
notice the privileges of physical mobility and
good health, until one day we are awakened
by an illness, an injury, or something larger,
a bereavement.

The Jewish memorial prayer, recited many
times while grieving, actually consists of an
affirmation of the beauty and sanctity of
life. Normally, we do not keep this aware-

ness at the forefront of our minds. The younger we are, the more likely we are to take only a fleeting glimpse from this perspective and then get back to everything we have to do. But loss bids us to become cognizant of the most ordinary pleasures and to be glad for every physical capacity we still retain. It is as though we begin to live the memorial prayer.

Early one morning, I approached the entry to a McDonald's in downtown Seattle and encountered a woman as she was coming out. She seemed to be in her mid-fifties, like me, and was pulling along a battered suitcase. She had several plastic bags draped from her arms and some clothes slung over the top of the suitcase. She mostly kept her head down, and so I only got a glance at her face. This particular McDonald's happens to be near a women's shelter, but her plastic bags and her weariness are what gave her away. I wanted to know where she was heading without a home to go to, and how she would spend the rest of the day.

I could not get this woman out of my mind. For the rest of the morning, I pondered her fate as compared to mine. What accident of good fortune had separated my story from hers? Something in her posture had told me she had known better days. I wondered if alcohol had robbed her of family and friends who would have taken her in. Perhaps mental illness had blockaded both jobs and relationships. Later that afternoon, I asked a circle of elders whether gratitude plays much of a role in their lives. A 69-year-old woman in a wheelchair declared, "I am grateful for all the bad things that have never happened to me." She had raised nine children on her own after a divorce, and endured multiple health problems. Now in an assisted-living residence, she told me her life is amply blessed in having a roof over her head, decent food to eat, and people in her life who care about her. The others readily concurred.

When I was in second grade, I went to a classmate's house after school one day. I entered a smelly, shabby chaos of clothes, toys, boxes, newspapers, and broken furniture that was her living room. She proudly took me up to her room. Her carpet was full of stains where I could see it, under the crushed crayons and other debris. Her dolls were naked and dirty, strewn around the room along with moldy sandwich crusts. In a mound on her bed was a torn blanket with the stuffing coming out. I had never imagined a house like this. Tugging at her sad blanket, I managed to smooth it out, and then I puffed up her pillow and tucked it under the blanket in a neat line. "See how nice it looks?" Just as I said this, I noticed her mother standing in the doorway. I saw that I had shamed her.

For years, I thought of this girl's house and her mother's look when I made my bed each morning and when I wrapped myself in my fresh, clean comforter at night. It was disturbing to have learned that there are mothers who are helpless. Why couldn't she make the house nice? The knowledge that everything is relative had taken hold of me, even though I did not yet have the words for this kind of recognition. I saw that everyone did not have the same life. There was an awareness of the contrasting under-side to things that I would carry from then on.

Gratitude is all about contrast. It is a state of mind wrought out of awareness of the many ways it is possible to suffer. With a change of fortune, we know that most of what we cherish can be lost — but this consciousness is not automatic. There is an element of choice in it, of deciding to keep paying attention and counting our bless-ings. Over time, we can cultivate this aware-ness by extending our compassion toward the anguish of others. In doing so, we can better appreciate where we stand and what we possess.

At the age of fifty-four, I was walking down rue Saint-Lazare in Paris when I pictured my grandmother cooking for the Passover Seder. Her legs would get heavy and painful, like pieces of wood, and yet she went on preparing the feast, year after year, well into her sixties. That morning in Paris my legs had been aching with our familial circulation trouble, and so I was not simply remembering my beloved grandmother — I was there, inhabiting her legs as she leaned up against the counter for support and finely grated a dozen carrots for the *tsimmis.*

Physical limitation contains its opposite — freedom — because it jars us into prizing that which we can still do. Our capacities, like standing at a stove for hours, go largely unrecognized until threatened. Every August when I go backpacking with my husband and a friend, both about ten years older than I am, we are among the most spirited people out on the trail. We are not counting the hours until we get to our destination, nor are we concerned about attaining an impressive number of miles. We are doing it. We are out there.

A friend in her early sixties has severe arthritis in her hands. She takes care of frail women in their eighties who have lost their way through dementia. Her hands sometimes make it hard for her to accomplish simple tasks, but the women are in no hurry. They are delighted by her humor and kindness, and they love the meals she places before them that are prepared with unfailing thoughtfulness. Alone in her house, my friend sometimes has to force away fears about her own future; but with the ladies, she feels the flush of every competence she continues to enjoy.

On rue Saint-Lazare, I recalled standing beside my grandmother in her kitchen when she announced that the next day's Seder would be the last one held at her apartment. She showed me the secrets of making the matzoh balls fluffy and keeping the brisket tender for the *tsimmis,* as well as ways to enrich the chicken soup so that it is brimming with flavor. She emphasized tiny details, repeating them over and over, making sure I was paying attention. I was in my thirties, with young uncomplaining legs. I fought back tears, honored by the instruction that had been passed along for centuries, while grieving the passing of an era in the life of my family.

Now I am a grandmother with aching legs, doing all that Passover cooking. My granddaughter Sophie calls out for more matzoh balls, just like I did at the age of eight — until she is so full she has trouble breathing. Amelia piles *charoset* on her plate in a mountain befitting a 6-year-old, and Maisie at four sucks her thumb after two portions of gefilte fish. They are finished long before the main course, as I always was. I picture their faces as I prepare for the Seder, especially when the pain in my legs creeps close to agony at nightfall on the days spent cooking since dawn.

In the five decades leading up to this moment in Paris, I surely had appreciated my grandmother's hard labor and dedication, but grasping the many dimensions of her endurance had waited for my own pain from standing too long. We do this kind of obscuring with our parents and grandparents until we experience enough of life to see them more fully. As young adults, we are sure that we know all we need to know about them. Then, somewhere in our thirties and forties, we start to get glimpses of our parents and grandparents as actual people in the world. This is the beginning of knowing them beyond the role they played for us, recognizing the context surrounding what they gave.

It was not until my mid-thirties that it occurred to me to ask my mother what her disappointments had been in her marriage to my father. She was startled. I was asking woman-to-woman, not as the daughter who always took her father's side in their relentless conflicts. She replied as a woman might to a good friend. It was my turn to be startled. There was so much to her side of the story that I had never imagined or even assigned potential sympathy. Her tone was without acrimony, because she heard no accusation in my voice and manner. I just wanted to know, and she just wanted to tell me. Twenty years later, as I write this account of the conversation, I more fully understand the relief I heard in her voice at finally being perceived.

Some of us must wait until a parent is in an intensive care unit before we can shed the illusion of their invincibility. Then we create a new relationship on the spot, even if it lasts only a few hours or weeks. Both parties become more visible to each other through the approach of death, the one curled in the hospital bed and the other seeing this sight. Things tend to get said that have never been ventured before. A kiss on the forehead, a hand held tenderly — such gestures seem to come from depths beyond our grievances. Although the relationship cannot cast off its history and be free of complications, this may be the clearest view of each other that has yet been possible.

A year before she died, my mother and I were having an argument. I no longer remember all the details of what we were fighting about, but I remember her warning me, "You're going to feel guilty after I'm gone." She was right, and she knew she was right because of a conflict she and my grandmother had been embroiled in immediately prior to my grandmother's death. We more readily embrace someone's view when the person is no longer around to insist upon it. When it is too late, applying compassion to a parent's stance is so much easier. This is what my mother knew and what we all learn after parents die.

Gratitude toward parents, in its fullest contours, is almost always belated. Long after a parent has died, understanding keeps on coming. The parent's fragile inner self, the essential innocence we all carry, becomes more and more apparent. We seem to need the distance of death to look beyond the parent's outer crust. Thus, we see in retrospect that the parent never was all-powerful and that all along there was an aching vulnerability, a need to be assured of being loved.

We realize how helpless our parents had been during our youthful experimentation — how they tried to warn us against foolish choices, how our petulance silenced them, how they thought about little else when we were off taking those many risks without thinking about them at all. Parenting never has been fair. We love our children far more than they love us, and in doing so we realize how dearly we were loved by our parents.

To see our parents' flaws in the context of their full humanity is to see our own imperfections in a more forgiving light. All at once, we see that the trials and errors we incurred while finding our own way have been as necessary as they were inevitable, especially in the realm of parenting. There are no perfect parents; the best are those who strive to correct their mistakes. As parents ourselves, we find that we must tangle with ordinary impatience, occasional exhaustion, unwitting repetitions of past hurts and outbursts from as yet unexplored parts of ourselves. On top of this, there are the many life circumstances that impinge on our best intentions — job stresses, money problems, untimely losses.

Later, we can only look into the eyes of our grown children and hope for eventual understanding. We know our presence in their lives preceded their earliest memories; they loved us before they had words, and so we remain larger than both language and life. We remember how hard it is to see a parent's hurt and how long it took us to reach something like gratitude.

In my late forties, I spent time in an area of Nepal without plumbing or electricity. Ever since, I have been aware of how wonderful it is to turn on a faucet instead of hauling water with a pail, or to turn on a stove instead of gathering firewood and tending a flame. Gratitude is a skill that must be nurtured, like any other. I am thankful when things work out well, and I am grateful for each day when hardship does not befall me. Having a blanket with seams intact and an orderly house remain recognized attributes of my life. Year by year, if I continue to accept the gifts of awareness that are accumulating, aging will grant me more and more appreciation.

My aunt and mother did take turns hosting the Seder, but gradually the ritual of everyone gathering together for Passover died away. The cousins scattered and had their own families. By the time my grandmother died, we already knew that it was not going to happen again — not like that, not with everyone together, not ever again. Before my legs give out, I hope that someday each of my granddaughters will stand beside me in the kitchen and learn the art of making matzoh balls that keep their shape in the boiling water yet are fluffy inside, and *tsimmis* so tender that a knife is not necessary for cutting the meat.

3

THE GREAT LEVELING

> I'm Nobody! Who are you? Are you —
> Nobody — too?
>
> EMILY DICKINSON

The quest to be *somebody,* to stand out from the crowd, can become injurious to the spirit. As early as kindergarten, we notice that certain kids are more sought-after than others and we begin to compare ourselves to them. These comparisons become a tyranny in adolescence, telling us whom we should seek out and whom we should scorn. We may then spend much of our adulthood in the dogged accrual of resources and accomplishments that would seem to set us above the rest, or we suffer from their nonattainment. If we secure some kind of status, we usually do not grant ourselves the peace of savoring what we have achieved. There is always someone we know who is doing so much better than we are.

A woman celebrating her sixtieth birthday attested to the burden of these strivings, once she had cast them off: "One of the great things about aging has been taking things easier, loosening up. I'm not so goal-oriented, not clawing my way anywhere anymore. I'm just looking to see what's out there. I have been getting connected with people I wouldn't otherwise have bothered to know."

Aging becomes a profound equalizer as getting older reveals what we hold in common. We see through the arbitrary divisions and designations of status, realizing that the only real difference between people is how readily we each embrace our shared humanity. Life gets so much lighter.

At our twentieth college reunion, I was among eight women who happened to sit together at our class luncheon. We had known each other only obliquely years back, but soon we were describing how depressed we had all been in our sophomore year. At the time, we had each been sure everyone else was doing really well. Externals are so deceiving. We took turns describing our envy of one another while in the midst of our private misery.

They told me, "You looked so free and happy, riding off on your bicycle with your knapsack, poncho, and long hair flowing." I admitted that I had actually been so desolate that I was unable to get my reading done unless I went for a long bike ride. For every two hours out in the Connecticut countryside, I was able to get an hour's worth of endorphin-derived concentration. As each of us confessed, it got funnier and funnier. We ended up laughing until we were weeping and our stomachs were aching.

To be able to laugh our hearts out like this, we had to be in our forties and in another phase entirely. We needed to be far enough away from our travail to meet it head on and not fear what it told us about ourselves. The weight of that loneliness, the wretched adrift feeling at the cusp of our twenties, was still vivid, but the poignancy finally had words. We each left the luncheon glowing, having discovered that our humiliations and insecurities had not been ours alone.

As the years pass, fissures slowly open in our facades. We get occasional glimpses into each other's inner realities — a friend's unburdening, a remarkably open conversation with a stranger on the train, a passage in a novel that hits home. Other people's stories work on us. We suspect that even our deepest shame is likely to be shared. It is a relief to see how little uniqueness there is in our self-doubts. Since other people struggle in similar ways, we realize it might be wiser to relent on these criticisms of ourselves.

A woman in her late forties recalled overhearing another woman's personal outpouring to her hairdresser a few chairs over:

She said she felt like such a fake. She went to work every day dressed to the nines but felt totally inadequate around her colleagues. She was fooling everyone into thinking she had it all together. I could hear it in her voice, how fragile she actually felt. My heart was breaking for her. I wanted to jump out of my chair and tell her it was the same for me, but I didn't have the guts. I just clung to her every word. I wondered how many of us out there feel like imposters, worrying about being found out. I won't ever forget her. It's so ironic — I gained a big chunk of confidence because of her.

As we age, anxiety loses its potency and its easing begins to free us. Quietly, almost imperceptibly, we gather in what can be known about difficulties we all endure. We learn that no one is endowed with absolute confidence and few are able to enact their goals as originally conceived. We see that compromising on our dreams does not signify defeat, and that flexibility with our hopes is not the same as giving up. We appreciate how pivotal it is to adapt to the unforeseen, to let fortuitous shifts lead us in new directions.

As the reunion was coming to a close, one of the women from the luncheon took me aside and said I was the person she had most admired at college. I insisted that this was impossible. She countered, "You followed your own star. I watched you taking courses according to your interests, not so it would look good for graduate school. I felt too afraid to do that." I was astonished. I said I had envied her for seeming to know where she was going, how her sails were full to the wind while I felt like a shipwreck. I admitted I had been jealous of her throughout our four years together. We stared at each other. *If only we had known.*

Somewhat over seventy, Sybil Macapia lives alone in a primitive cabin on the edge of the wilderness. She hauls water every morning from her barn to the cabin and chops wood for her stove. She does not mind using an outhouse. Her garden hose permits bathing outdoors in summer and her stove gives her hot water for bathing indoors in winter. Electricity and a phone, along with her car, link her to a small town nearby. "When I was young," she told a local reporter, "my ego worked really hard to establish my particular brand of extraordinariness." She continued:

> I'm no longer concerned with who I am — I don't, in fact, believe that there is a "who I am." I don't get caught up in it . . . I am so gleefully common as mud. There's nothing to protect; I can just relax about it. . . . It's very liberating to realize that I'm not special at all, that I am just a grain of human sand among all.[1]

As our bloated opinion of ourselves deflates, our well-being expands. In stark contrast, some people try to cling to what they perceive as their superiority and try to prop themselves up with symbols of distinctiveness and status. Where they reside, what they wear, who they know — these things attest to their high standing in relation to others. There is no rest from the effort to maintain or exceed their position, even as whispers from an aging body remind them of all they have in common with everyone else.

A woman who had become ill in her mid-sixties reached the point where she could no longer take care of herself. She needed help with almost every task of daily life, including using the bathroom and getting in and out of bed. She was wealthy enough to hire full-time aides, but would order them around with such blistering barbs that soon every employee of the home health agency refused to take care of her. No amount of extra money could induce these workers to be in this woman's presence.

I sat with her in her palatial house and discussed arrangements for moving to a nursing home. Suddenly, she realized there was no way she could purchase the many varieties of kindness that were necessary for staying in her own home. She begged me to give her one more chance — to teach her how to treat her helpers differently so that they would agree to take care of her.

I was intrigued by her proposal. Could decency be acquired at the last minute? This woman was being catapulted into change out of necessity, but I was not sure she could stop perceiving those who changed her sheets as beneath her. Could she adopt a respectful tone regardless of her attitude? Despite these doubts, I decided it was fair to take her at her word and try to create this opportunity.

The home health supervisor who had spent many years as an in-home caregiver agreed to take care of her, with certain conditions. "Come off your high horse," she told the physically fragile woman. "Speak to me like one person to another, not like a servant. Pretend we are equals. Words like *please* and *thank you* will be music to my ears. Remember — if you say one rude word to me, the deal is off." We arranged for a monthlong trial period, at the end of which her care would be passed on to a regular worker if she mastered these basic courtesies and showed a change in her attitude.

Within a few months' time, the two became buddies. The supervisor insisted on continuing to do most of the care herself, saying that she had never received so much praise and heartfelt gratitude. The formerly domineering woman told me, "It's a good thing you didn't just write me off. I would never have known what is to have a friend like this." A year later, she was able to die in her own home knowing this well.

■ ■ ■ ■

I once turned down a job that would have tripled my salary and dramatically increased my cachet in the world. Almost thirty, I was working part-time as a social worker at a community clinic in downtown Seattle. The new job would have been full time, in the public eye, and full of commensurate pressures. I would have lost the two and a half days a week I had set aside for writing a book. I had no contract or any assurance that one day the manuscript would be published, but work on it was as meaningful as anything I had ever done. On the phone, when I told the high-placed executive that I needed to preserve my writing time, she called me crazy and meant it.

In our society, what is heralded as the "good" life is clear. We are supposed to partake in the zeal of succeeding, which is measured by our capacity to purchase. To follow other convictions, such as acquiring as little as possible or seeking to manifest our creativity regardless of remuneration, means enduring the burdens of deviance. In some circles, we may be accused of being un-American or at least not normal.

A painter in his mid-fifties recalled his

agonized struggle in his twenties and thirties to maintain his artistic integrity. Working fervently on his paintings whenever he could, he lived off his tips as a waiter. He had frequent spells of despair, especially when he would compare himself to his college classmates who had pursued lucrative careers and were doing well by society's standards.

My parents wrote me off, but the worst part was thinking I was a failure myself. Somehow I kept on painting, but it was hell. Then something clicked inside me when I was turning forty. I was done with all of that hand-wringing and putting myself down. I decided this was my life and I was going to accept it. I just wish this had come to me sooner. I've been pretty content ever since, even though I still only get a show here and there.

More than most, artists have to shut out the noise of the dominant culture that insists on more practical pursuits. Some go for years without assurance that their work matters to anyone but themselves, enduring long periods of poverty in order to concentrate on painting, writing, or making music. For them, everything depends on holding firm to their belief in the worth of their craft.

Similarly, those who wish to instruct the young or serve the poor have to contend with being near the bottom rung in terms of pay and public veneration. While scant honor may be accorded them, teachers and social workers hold our children's self-esteem and our most vulnerable families' self-respect in their hands. Those who thrive in such endeavors must actively nurture their conviction that their work is of highest value, since they receive so much less materially than what their work actually merits.

A key payoff comes later in life. The mirage of power and money fades for everyone as death approaches, and the last may truly become first. They may go on deriving satisfaction from their work long after those involved in less fulfilling pursuits move into a belated search for meaning. With new respect from the same people who once pitied their relatively meager circumstances, they may end up heralded as models for aging with dignity and purpose due to having lived for years in accordance with a well-satisfied spirit.

I am glad that I have kept on writing. I see how almost forty years of a writer's discipline is embedded in the way I live.

Who knows? These quiet habits may stand me in good stead through the vagaries of life yet to come.

When she was in her late forties, a woman who had spent years developing a successful business became depressed. "It was like a seesaw — the more my outer life went up, the more my inner life went down." She began reading the Christian mystics, an interest she had abandoned while fulfilling her outer ambitions. She came across a sentence, "Your adversary is your helper." This startled her into realizing that she needed to listen to what her depression was telling her about her life:

> When I was younger I had this unquestioning belief in the importance of achievement. This idea became the illusion that drove my life. Now when I look back I see it was all a kind of con job I did on myself. That's the strange thing: I totally believed that the meaning of life was nothing more than getting the job done well and earning other people's approval.[2]

She ended up leaving the glamour of her lavish lifestyle behind and attending graduate school to study comparative religion.

Returning to her spiritual leanings, doing what she loved, released her from her suffering.

In our youth, we are afraid lest anyone see our doubts and insecurities. Self-importance is exhausting. As we get older, our shame diminishes or comes to seem pointless. Once we see how much company we have in our difficulties, we give our humiliations less weight in our own reckoning and we are more apt to be open about our weaknesses. To welcome being "common as mud" brings us closer to true contentment. We have much less inclination to be judgmental, to scorn others, or to find fault. We are far less impressed by how much money someone has made or how many professional accolades they have piled up. To be wealthy in relationships comes to seem the most valuable kind of fortune. Who is *somebody* and who is *nobody?* We recognize that we are all essentially the same when it comes to living and dying, and it is a relief.

4
RELATIONSHIPS

It is idle, having planted an acorn in the morning, to expect that afternoon to sit in the shade of the oak.

ANTOINE DE SAINT-EXUPÉRY

Through a sibling bond, friendship, or pairing as a couple, longevity in a relationship gives us rootedness in a shared past. We are well acquainted with each other's insecurities and tribulations, allowing us to look back and laugh at earlier foibles. We can probe the twists and turns of each other's lives, making sense of what has happened so much more easily in unison than we could with solitary rumination. Many things do not need to be said, and a great deal can be understood with just a grunt or a nod. When closeness deepens with the passage of years, long-standing relationships become an irreplaceable bounty in later life.

A woman in her late fifties said of her

older sister, "Somewhere along the line we became the same age," guessing that this occurred when she achieved equal footing by striking out on her own at the age of eighteen. Her sister, four years the elder, disagreed. She claimed that it was not until both reached midlife. "Now I feel there's no age difference, except when we fall back into old roles — like when I become the bossy older sister."

Improvements in the way we regulate our emotions may make our relationships better overall. As we get older, we may become more skillful in the arts of compromise and consonance. Fighting more fairly, we may no longer stoop so low during arguments. Saying what we mean more directly, we may set aside pride and express our needs more clearly than when we were younger. Having become more self-aware, we may speak up about our needs more readily and pay greater attention to the ways we obstruct others' preferences. As elders, we tend to choose our conflicts more carefully and tolerate mixed feelings with less distress. Brain scans reveal that we tend to become less reactive to negative situations with age, confirming that we are better equipped for well-being in relationships than ever.[1]

■ ■ ■ ■

Nothing is guaranteed between siblings — neither friendliness nor allegiance. A 95-year-old woman told me she had not spoken to her younger sister for over forty years, ever since her sister had made off with the family heirlooms shortly after their mother's funeral. Stories of lifelong rifts are plentiful, but so also are accounts of sibling friendships that only get better with the passage of time.

A 55-year-old woman was furious when her older sister insisted she would not go to visit their dying mother in the hospital: "How could she put her resentment above Mom's last wishes? I can't believe such selfishness." Her 61-year-old sister did call their mother to ask about her condition, but would not relent on her refusal of face-to-face contact. Their mother later died without a farewell from her firstborn child.

In this instance, their mother's father had committed suicide a few months before she held her first baby in her arms. This means that the older sister grew up with a devastated mother who hardly ever got out of bed, while six years later the younger one had a mother who sang to her and often took her to the zoo. The older one may recount years of alienation and loneliness, while the younger one may depict an entirely loving, even joyful atmosphere in the family. It is no wonder that this mother and firstborn daughter had been unable to undo the effects of an emotional barrier that had become deeply entrenched. Both had been robbed by the timing of the suicide, causing them to miss opportunities for closeness that would not come again.

Getting older can help us perceive siblings with greater sympathy. When prompted to compare her sister's early years to her own, the younger sister was taken aback. She realized that their formative years bore no relation to each other: "It's as though we were raised by different mothers." All at once, she understood that her older sister deserved respect for the decency of her phone calls to the hospital, and that her lack of visiting did not warrant scorn.

There are as many truths as there are members of a family. Birth order and personality produce distinct angles of perception, as does the family's situation at the time of each sibling's birth. Many siblings do not stop to consider how their family's circumstances may have differed when each was young, especially if they are close in age. Thus, two sisters who grew up in the same room in the same house may tell two completely different versions of their family story, and both versions will be accurate in terms of their respective experiences.

Grasping the power of such disparate standpoints within families is never more important than when siblings come together to assist frail parents at the end of their lives. Grudges and resentments that had been kept under the surface for years may rise up with particular intensity at these junctures. This is when it is hardest and most necessary to respect each other's truth and find a way to turn anger into sympathy.

At forty-eight, a firstborn son who had been close to his mother all of his life stepped in with extra help immediately after she had a stroke. "I call her a lot — several times a day — just to check on her. Before, it was just a quick call in the morning, but now I worry about her all the time." His 45-year-old sister soon quit her job in another state and moved into their mother's home to take care of her:

Here I am doing her laundry, cleaning her house, getting her groceries, paying her bills, you name it — yet all I ever hear is how great my brother is. The sun has always risen and set over my brother's head, so this is nothing new. It's just hard to take right now. You'd think she would notice how much I'm doing for her.

A few months before she died, smaller strokes worsened their mother's frailty. She became dependent on her daughter for the fundamental tasks of daily life. The daughter was often up in the middle of the night helping her mother to the bathroom. Once, near the end, her mother seized her hand and said, "What would I do without you? You're an angel." The tender acknowledgment meant everything. The daughter felt the sun rise over her head. During the last night's vigil, she held her tiny mother in her arms as she slept. "I'm so glad I took care of her. She got to see who I am. And my brother actually respects me now."

Experiences like these can revive sibling bonds later in life, especially when the intensity of old resentments diminishes as siblings move on with their lives. The "favorites" endure difficulties like everyone else, and those who felt disadvantaged earlier tend to find ample rewards outside the family later on. Life has a way of evening things out, at the same time that early unfairness in the family of origin recedes in importance.

Best of all is when siblings become friends. Then there is the double comprehension of being from the same family and having known one another since the beginning. The highest levels of understanding are possible, despite the complications of different familial truths. A 54-year-old man with one sister five years older and one five years younger described their being more dependent on each other at this point in their lives:

My sisters and me, these aren't high-maintenance relationships. It's just that whenever we're together, we keep going. We don't need to weed or prune, we just go on from where we left off. . . . We have more contact and more reasons for talking, about my mother's health, about our lives, because the families we made are gone. [My sister's] kids have families of their own now, and there's her divorce, too. And mine, of course. We've got more time.[2]

Old friends know our stories. They can attest to the ways we have surmounted past difficulties, while comprehending what still dogs us. They are familiar with such a broad swath of our lives that their very presence may prompt a wider perspective, dislodging us from a stuck position or renewing our patience with the pace of change. With their comprehensive knowledge of our prior life experiences, they may also be able to cajole us beyond the concerns that currently pre-occupy us.

In a real sense, old friends grant us views of ourselves that we cannot obtain on our own. As we narrate an ongoing quandary, telling one jagged edge of the tale after the next, such friends enable us to gain insights by drawing parallels to our earlier struggles. We may be able to discern certain continuities, to value the strengths we have acquired along the way, and begin to feel something like coherence.

The timeless quality old friends feel upon being reunited derives from having once been young together. Time itself seemed to move differently back then. Experiences lasted longer and loomed larger. A friend from youth can bring us back through the decades to a key event in a rush of feeling and memory, as if it happened yesterday. Recollections held in common thus fill a great storehouse from which understanding can be drawn and sense can be made.

Old friends can also raise questions about tough issues that we might resist if posed by an intimate partner. With a different stake emotionally, a friend may allow us to think out loud and test ideas without worrying about the impact of what we are saying. Couples often evolve a host of topics each may not be able to hear dispassionately from the other, while friends can grant each other the freedom of wide-ranging, unimpeded exploration. Such friends may also offer perspective from the years preceding the partner's arrival, supplying reminders of what was carried into the relationship from the past and cannot be blamed on the partner.

As time passes, we may notice aspects of an old friend we never appreciated before. Fresh areas of inquiry and conversation may open up. Each one's gains in life experience may enliven the dialogue and propel the give-and-take to new depths. Friends who get to grow old together often discover further dimensions of friendship.

Sadly, it is also possible to gauge our own growth by noticing the ways an old friend has not advanced. Divergent viewpoints that once did not matter may have widened into a gulf, or we may find that a trait admired thirty years ago now seems less impressive. Even when realizing that we have grown apart from an old friend, we may choose to persist in such long-standing relationships out of the recognition that they are irreplaceable and still contain the wealth of a shared past.

A single woman reached her mid-forties with several loyal friends. Her childhood and adolescence had been lonely, and so she knew the worth of kind companionship. She had always been the one to offer child care in a pinch, to bring over meals when a friend was sick, or to give a ride when a friend's car was in the shop. Her one failing in the art of friendship was in being unable to let others know when she needed help. At her core, she saw herself as a solitary traveler, a loner whose path diverged from how others lived.

When she got breast cancer at the age of forty-six, her friends rallied around her. They took turns accompanying her to chemotherapy, cleaning her house, preparing meals, and walking her dog. She discovered that her life was rich in relationships. During and after her cancer treatment, her conception of herself shifted. She saw that her life was fully animated by friends who were like family, and that growth for her consisted in allowing herself to count on others and receive their nurturance. This revelation carried her forward without fear for her future.

I was twenty years old when a colleague in his forties gave me a ride to an off-site staff meeting. He was an accomplished person whom I admired. At a stoplight, I asked him why he had chosen to go back into psycho-therapy, a decision he had just confided in me. He replied with a single sentence: "I want to learn how to love."

I was perplexed. The idea that we need to learn how to love had never occurred to me. I thought romantic love, especially, was something you fell into and out of, and that it just happened. It was also alarming that he still considered himself a novice at such an advanced age.

At that time, the idea of two people being *meant* for each other held great sway with me. There were issues of timing, attraction, availability, and fate, but it seemed it was mostly a matter of finding the right person. Once two such people found each other, they would be all set for spending the rest of their lives together.

By my late twenties, I often thought back to that moment at the stoplight with aching sympathy. I had discovered that intimacy is complicated. Clothing can be removed and motions can be made, but emotional nakedness is another realm entirely. The capacity to trust and be vulnerable to another person is hard to develop and is easily damaged. Lovers bring out the best and the worst in each other, and it can be a wild ride until surging emotions are sorted out.

Intimacy commences once the commitment is made to stay together — then the work begins. It is tempting to abandon intimate relationships when the work becomes strenuous. A partner's faults are easy to see, but the obstacles we put in a partner's way may remain unseen and unacknowledged. Our original experiences with counting on those who took care of us as children can get mixed up in this return to vulnerability. Many people feel like "damaged goods" and are too ashamed to tell their partners about bad memories that keep getting in the way. Meanwhile, each partner may accuse the other of causing pain that actually stems from internal sources.

The capacity to put aside the convenience of blame, delving instead into further self-awareness, tends to require years of practice and perseverance. Couples who have been together for a long time find that they resolve their conflicts more easily and leave less of a hurt residue. A 64-year-old man described an evolution that had occurred during almost forty years of marriage:

> When we have a fight, we're both more ready than ever to give in and get back to living our lives. We know how far we can push an argument — what's worth it and what's not. It seems as though we've been through every conceivable dispute a hundred times already, so why bother going to extremes? I get much less upset than I used to, and things get resolved much faster. This is one of the great rewards for sticking with a relationship for a long time.

Intimacy advances when both people convey their needs openly, rather than disguising them beneath grabs for power or false independence. A relationship cannot succeed fully until both people become interested in finding out what it is about themselves that is presenting difficulties for the other. Often, one must take the lead and shoulder a greater share of introspection and honesty for a while, until the other person finally accepts the necessity of looking within. Then a relationship begins to ascend to the level of true mutuality.

The sexual realm mirrors what is going on in the relationship as a whole. We become better lovers as these barriers drop away and the passion of trust increases. Secrets and hurts are released from their lonely concealment. We store up minute knowledge of each other's needs. As emotional generosity increases outside the bedroom, attentiveness and joy expand in lovemaking. Eventually, a couple's sense of emotional resonance may culminate in an exquisite kind of surrender. A 64-year-old woman described her relationship with her 70-year-old partner:

> Over the years we've changed. We've slowed down some. It takes longer; it takes patience and gentle caring. We've always been able to talk to each other about making love. . . . We do more foreplay, and it's a lot more fun. It's very relaxed. We can talk together about what gives us pleasure, what we want more of and less of. This is important to both of us. This part of our lives is very special.[3]

The sweetness of intimacy keeps growing. In later life, bodies may become creaky and the mechanics of who does what, for how long, and in what location may change, but the most important aspects of being together improve. Long-standing partners tend to let down whatever of their guard is left. Such couples talk more openly, laugh more readily, and become more inventive about the ways they seek to please each other.

Over the years, closeness builds upon itself. A couple gradually becomes more fluent in the language of each other's feelings, particularly ways of grieving. Each knows how to comfort the other — when to be especially tender and attentive, and when to allow room for solitude. This mutual sensitivity becomes especially valuable when the couple goes through difficult transitions, such as leaving behind a beloved house or facing the death of an old friend.

Couples in their eighties and nineties have assured me that reaching later life within a thriving relationship is well worth the considerable effort. They claim that their visceral knowledge of each other, combined with a long history together and deepening trust, is as romantic as it gets.

The sight of an older couple walking hand in hand has always enchanted me. My gaze is pulled to the ease of their affection, the attunement of their gait, the companionable silence in their posture. I am most moved by those who seem to be taking nothing for granted, savoring the pleasure of being together and celebrating through every gesture that they are both still here.

As a child, I wondered how a couple who had been together all of their lives could stand to lose each other. One of them would have to die first, I reasoned, and the other would be left alone. I distinctly recall thinking these thoughts. It is a memory of grasping unimaginable grief for the first time. I was seven or eight years old. I must have heard about someone dying and leaving behind their companion of a lifetime. My conception of a *lifetime* was then so huge that the loss I glimpsed was beyond all measurement, a reflection of its true immensity.

5
Loss

The heart of the wise is in the house of mourning.

ECCLESIASTES 7:4

Inside all of us is a great pool of grief that keeps enlarging as each fresh loss is added to the others. We often find ourselves weeping for old sorrows along with the new. Over the years, we learn how to dip into grief for a while and then step back out into the oxygen of love and life. It is not that we get good at it, but we know what we must do and we do it. Grieving does not get easier, but we acquire the skills to bear it and the wisdom to accede to its rhythms.

Vicki Kennedy, wife of the late Senator Ted Kennedy, was asked what it was like in the months before Ted died, both of them knowing that the end was near. "The only day he spent in bed was the day he died," she replied. "He was keeping us all going. It wasn't a sad time — it was a beautiful time."[1]

Having done it so many times before, we become confident about our eventual emergence from even the deepest sorrow. We understand how necessary it is to cherish, rather than fear, the sadness that arises when we are swamped by memories of someone we have lost. The sadness passes, and the remembering becomes sweet. Our spirit for life returns with knowing how to gather in every kind of solace. Appreciation for the presence of those still here with us becomes acute. We become determined to make the most of the time we have left with one another, to turn mourning into attentiveness.

I was fortunate to have attained the age of eighteen before experiencing my first death. It was in early May of my senior year of high school. At the age of sixty-five, my German teacher dropped dead of a heart attack. *Mrs. Martello died this morning.* The message reached me shortly after I returned home from school on the day she had been absent for the first time. I dropped to the kitchen floor and wailed. My mother stood there helplessly, having never seen her older daughter fall apart like this.

Mrs. Martello was not like other teachers. She had replaced the iron desks with less constricting tables, and put Joni Mitchell and Simon and Garfunkel on the record player while we endured our grammar exercises. She wore huge pendant earrings and colorful vests. She talked to us as though we were equals, not subjects, which was even more thrilling than getting rid of the desks. Once, she mentioned having been tortured by the Nazis when she was in the French Resistance, and we always assumed this explained her pronounced limp and her drooping right eyelid.

Scorning the teacher's broad oak desk, she would sit atop one of the tables and read Rilke out loud to us. Most of us could not understand the poems at all, whether conveyed through the impassioned music of our teacher's native German or quietly in translation. I did grasp a word here and there during her readings, but was mostly intrigued by the sight of my wild teacher rocking back and forth. She showed us that there was a reward ahead for persisting with this impossible language.

A year after her death, I got a summer job working at Haus Hohenfried, a children's home in southern Bavaria. The town was so remote that few people spoke English. I had decided to honor my teacher's memory by immersing myself in the German language and forcing it into my reluctant brain once and for all.

About six weeks into my stay there, my beloved teacher came to me in a dream that seemed to last all night long:

Mrs. Martello is sitting at the edge of my bed, looking exactly as she did before — wearing those same flamboyant earrings and a vest. I tell her everything that has happened since she died. We both know that she is dead, but we make no mention of it. She asks me what I am doing in Bavaria, just a few miles from the ruin of Eagle's Nest, Hitler's favorite stronghold. I tell her how I can finally chitchat in German and even eavesdrop on the older staff talking fondly about the good old days of the Third Reich. She laughs, her head thrown back in that familiar way. I tell her how I dread choosing a major soon at college, and she declares, "Follow your curiosity. Don't get boxed in. Forget about earning a living. Just learn, learn, learn." We go on like this for hours, our dialogue full of lively exchanges. Suddenly, we hear the chimes of the clock downstairs at the children's home, signaling that it is time for me to wake up. I plead, "No! No! Stay just a little longer! Please!" She starts fading, bidding me farewell, and vanishes.

I woke up sobbing. I knew it was just a dream, but I felt as though I had been actually talking with a living person. I hastened to record what she had said in my journal. "Does it matter whether or not she was really with me?" I asked myself then, and I still wonder now. For years, I have carried this conversation with me and have drawn on it for guidance during times of confusion and uncertainty.

Among older people, a topic that never fails to generate animated discussion begins with the question, "Have you ever had the experience of seeing or feeling the presence of someone you have lost?" Usually, one person is brave enough to describe seeing her husband in the hallway the day after he died, gazing at her with loving concern. Then, everyone else bursts in at the same time, trying to tell their story. A man in his nineties once described daily visits from his deceased wife: "She comes to me as a bird. Every morning, I'm telling you. She said she would. I always know which bird is her, even if there are a bunch of other birds around."

I have heard people from all walks of life produce these tales with intense emotion and considerable detail. Whether or not accounts like these are true in the normal sense of the word, such stories matter. Our mind obeys the summons of our heart and finds a means through which to assure us that our loved ones are still with us.

Grief heals when it is received by a caring other. Something so deep can be assuaged so simply, yet mourning requires us to be vulnerable in the presence of another, and this is not easy. Ancient Jewish tradition suggests that we are supposed to fall apart, to disintegrate, letting others take in our feelings as they tend to daily life tasks on our behalf. In the modern context, it can be difficult to find others willing to receive our grief with such an open heart while we let down our guard to this degree.

A 79-year-old man whose wife had Alzheimer's disease had not cried since he was a small boy. His face held deep lines of unexpressed grief. He was losing a little bit more of his wife of fifty-two years every day. Under protest, he finally agreed to attend a support group for spouses and partners in the same predicament. He said he would attend one meeting just to see how it was, but he could not imagine how it could possibly be of use. A week later, he described the experience:

I was the only man among seven women. A few minutes into the hour, one of the women started telling a story about being unable to get her husband to take a shower. She stopped mid-story, too choked up to continue, trying to tell us how fastidious her husband had always been. I heard a few of the other women crying in sympathy. I couldn't look at her. I put my head in my hands, and a tear went down my cheek and dropped onto my lap. It was so surprising to me. There was so much sadness, if I could have released it, but I couldn't.

He began attending the meetings regularly, and gradually the lines on his face softened. When I asked him why he kept returning to the group, he replied, "The women do my crying for me." It was as if the weeping women in the support group were releasing him from the prison of a lifetime of pent-up feelings. He said he always left the meetings feeling much lighter. His daughter told me that she had never seen him be so outwardly loving and expressive, feeling as if she was getting to know him on this level for the first time.

The women in the support group instructed him in the ways of grief. They told him he would have good and bad days, along with times when he would not feel the loss at all. Finding out that this wavelike movement was common to all grieving freed him from the guilt that kept him from ever leaving his wife in someone else's care. Once a month, he resumed going to the opera or the symphony with his best friends, aware that the ache of missing the woman he loved would ebb and flow. His job was to sustain himself for her sake. This is what the women said.

It is the nature of grief to change in form and intensity. Fortunately, we do not have a say in when it will surge and when it will recede. Months or sometimes years later, a certain song or a particular aroma reaches us and we experience a towering swell of sorrow. The grief breaks through, much more intensely than what we experienced in the weeks immediately following the loss. We are brought to tears, the sorrow pulls back, and we go on. The grieving we still have left to do finds us again when it must.

Several months after her husband died, a 66-year-old woman began to volunteer as a teacher's aide at a nearby elementary school. She had been worried about being unable to cry or experience anything deeply, as though a layer of gauze were between her and life. She felt like "one of the living dead." She hoped that getting out of the house a few mornings a week and being around children would renew her spirit.

One night, she was listening to the radio as she repaired the hem of a skirt she wanted to wear the next day. A song came on that had been the centerpiece of their courtship so many years before. She wept as she had never wept before in her life, for hours on end, and then fell asleep on the couch fully clothed. The next morning, she found the skirt across the room where she had flung it, the needle and thread still dangling from the unfinished hem.

As she walked to the school that morning, she smelled rain in the air and observed the drama of dark clouds overhead. She noticed the squawking of crows and watched one swoop by with a treat in its beak. During the lunch break, she told the story of her husband's death to another teacher's aide. This was the first time she had let anyone at the school know she had been so recently bereaved. Now the words came pouring forth, with a few tears. Over the next few weeks, her face took on its customary animation, replacing the blank look that had worried her friends. She became so ebullient with the children that the teachers were soon fighting over who got to have her in their classroom. Alive to her grief, she was available again for living.

From the vantage point of youth, sorrows in later life seem so relentless that we cannot imagine living through them. We watch elders lose dear friends and relatives, give up beloved houses, and relinquish cherished involvements. It can seem that later life is composed of interludes between disasters. What consolation could there be? We conclude that old age must be a dire time, indeed.

It is only later that we find that fresh life evolves out of each grief. We must open ourselves to sorrow, allow it to move through us, and await all that will grow out of it. The deeper the loss, the longer it takes to recognize how much of life still awaits us. Rather than trying to evade its intensity, we have to allow loss to animate the way we spend our days.

Isabel Allende wrote that the sorrow of losing her 28-year-old daughter was "a cleansing experience" in that she was thrown back to the essentials of living:

> Paralyzed and silent in her bed, my daughter Paula taught me a lesson that is now my mantra: You only have what you give. It's by spending yourself that you become rich. . . . She never had any money, but she needed very little. When she died she had nothing and she needed nothing. . . . Because of Paula, I don't cling to anything anymore. Now I like to give much more than I receive.[2]

Following a bereavement, we become keenly aware of those who are in distress. It is as though another sense has been acquired that leads us toward others in need of comforting. As we console others, we simultaneously honor the magnitude of our loss and the ways that grief has changed us. We carry the person we have lost with us in every act of re-engagement.

All that is wonderful in life comes with the possibility of its loss. How we carry this awareness divides those who live well from those who do not. As losses mount with the years, bitterness can exert an inexorable pull. Some people close up, pushing away anything that would risk their heart. New life beckons at times, but they keep to themselves. The door to change stays sealed. They shut out the very influences that would have brought them renewal. There can be regeneration after great sorrow, but only if we let the grief open us up to further life. The next portion of living is there for the taking, as soon as we are ready to find our way back to flourishing.

In the years since losing my beloved teacher, my list of deaths has grown long — my grandfather, grandmother, father-in-law, mother-in-law, father, mother, aunt, and uncle. This is what it means to live long — to grow more accustomed to outliving. What else is there to do? With each bereavement I have borne, each time I have been left emotionally bare by the rigors of loss, I have become more attentive to the constant interplay of fragility and strength, of fracturing and integration, that is essential to coming out the other side.

To grieve is to experience a relationship — a man said this to me after I had given a presentation about grief. He announced this happily, as though the very sentence gave him delight. I knew this was right, that the heartache is proportionate to the loving, but he had captured this truth in one triumphant phrase.

When I drop a matzoh ball into the boiling water, I see my grandmother's hands and a wave of grief comes over me. I remind myself what a privilege it was to have had a grandmother beyond my fortieth birthday, one who had the stamina to pass on the traditions when I was ready to receive them. To this day, when I savor Rilke's poems in the original German, I am certain there is a spirit world in which Mrs. Martello sees me reveling in her gift.

6
SPIRITUALITY

Two veils separate us from the divine —
health and security.

SUFI SAYING

When I became a therapist in my late twenties, I was surprised at how elders delved so readily into life's deepest questions. The young wanted to talk about interpersonal anguish — calamities in love, anger at parents — while older people wanted to figure out what life and death were all about. I learned that later life is when our most profound existential grappling occurs, especially following a fright like a heart attack or a stroke.

Any experience of woe can become a gateway to spirituality, but most powerful of all are the circumstances that render us helpless. We never forget an abject moment like waiting for someone to pull up our pants after being helped to reach the toilet.

We are dust, and to dust we shall return. Those who have never been religiously inclined and would not use words like *soul* or *faith* still get caught in the search for answers to our finitude and vulnerability. To understand our lives, we must seek a context for both our misery and the times of exhilaration we have known. We are drawn into a larger story.

A 64-year-old man explained that he had become increasingly aware of "the interconnectedness of everything" as the years passed. "I look out at dense green foliage and think of the fractal pattern in our brains, and how plants and animals are the same on a molecular level. Our individual selves are just the tip of everything we see. More and more, this point of view calms me and puts things in perspective."

At the age of nine, I came to the last page of Anne Frank's diary and read an italicized note that had been inserted at the end of the text. It said that Anne and everyone else in the attic hideaway had been taken away to concentration camps. I ran to my mother in great distress: "What are concentration camps?" With her reply in my heart, I ran back to my room, closed the door, and renounced God.

Sometime in my earlier childhood, I had arrived at deep faith in God's goodness. Talking to God was my secret practice, because no one else in my family mentioned prayer and I did not understand exactly what was going on in synagogue. But on this Saturday afternoon in the spring of 1963, I realized that there was no such thing as God, because the God to whom I had been so devoted would not abandon an innocent girl and her family.

Later, I studied religion and philosophy in college. Claiming to be an atheist, I became passionately engaged in religious dilemmas like theodicy, the problem of the existence of evil along with an all-powerful deity. I wanted to know how various cultures and traditions had explained suffering over the course of human history. Then, as I faced real life as a social worker, the unfair distribution of hardships only left me more perplexed. Was it random fate that led some to have more tragedies in their lives than others? How much of human difficulty stems from personal choices versus societal structures? Could it be that things happen for no reason? Why are we here?

At the age of thirty, I paged through the Talmud for the first time, a twenty-volume account of rabbinic arguments and counter-arguments going back a thousand years. Intrigued, I found in these discussions every question I had ever sought to pose, and hundreds more I had not yet pondered. It was embarrassing. The tradition I thought I had shed seemed to permeate my consciousness.

Unwittingly, my efforts to free myself of inherited practices had become a kind of reverse engagement. Art Spiegelman, the cartoonist, explained that he is culturally Jewish but "religiously not so much" and that he finds "comfort from the discomfort of being alienated from the religious rituals."[1] The Hebrew *Yis-ra-el* derives from root words that mean *wrestling with God.* I saw that I had never stopped arguing with God about the Holocaust.

Then, the man who would eventually become my husband invited me to attend Rosh Hashanah services with him. I had not been in a synagogue since leaving my parents' home. That night, the ancient melodies moved through me and brought tears to my eyes. I leaned up against Barry's shoulder and felt his tallis against my cheek. Long ago, the silk of my father's prayer shawl had been the perfect place in which to sink my face during sleepy Sabbath mornings in synagogue. I felt as though I had come home.

It takes a long time to learn to listen to the still, small voice within. We tend to seek direction outside ourselves, while our soul's language is drowned out by the commotion of external striving. It is possible to lose awareness of this inner voice for years and to be guided by the noisy dictates of other people's conceptions of a worthy life.

Suffering makes our need to hear what is within acute. A man was brought to his knees emotionally and financially when he discovered his wife had been having a long affair. He also learned that she had co-signed a huge loan for their alcoholic son behind his back. "I felt a ripping sensation as I let go of forty-five years together." He lost half of his retirement savings, and he was fifty percent liable for loan payments that his son was not honoring. Nothing about his situation felt fair. In his mid-sixties, he felt like Job standing alone on a barren rock.

While enduring a dark night of the soul, we feel as though everything that had once been definite has become uncertain. We wander around, unable to find our bearings. To be lost this way awakens primal fears about our capacity to survive, about who we really are and what we have to offer anyone. All relationships are open to question. It seems there is nothing to count on, that no one can be trusted completely.

In preindustrial times, when we only had fickle moonlight and firelight for illumination, darkness could be impenetrable. When I sleep in the woods, I sometimes douse the campfire and shut off my flashlight in order to join in this continuity with every person who has ever lived. There is a whisper of terror in darkness so absolute. My ears suddenly pick up every rustling leaf. No amount of reason and reassurance can quell what stems from our wild ancestry.

This man reached the very ground of existence, a despair that joined him with every person who had ever sorrowed. Each day, he thought about how much time he was likely to have left to live. Then it came to him. He decided to strip his life down to the barest essentials:

I realized all I needed was a place to live, food to eat, and clothes on my back. I was lucky to be still healthy and able-bodied. I certainly didn't need all those expensive gadgets. They were toys. I could use my woodstove for heat, and my garden could feed me in the summer. I had plenty of clothes. If some of my shirts got a bit ragged, the thrift shops make you a king for five bucks. How much money is in the bank is literally immaterial. I saw that I was actually a rich man. She hadn't taken that much from me, after all.

He started to unfurl the cocoon of bitterness in which he had wrapped himself, deciding to open up to life's possibilities as much as he could. The despair lifted.

By the time he was forty, Arthur Frank had gone through a serious heart attack and life-threatening cancer. "Alive but detached from everyday living, you can finally stop to consider why you live as you have," he declared on the first page of the book he wrote about his ordeal. As he emerged, he vowed to live in accordance with what he had learned. The book ends thus:

How strange and wonderful the world must have looked to Jonah, come out of the belly of that great fish. Could he preserve the poignancy of that first moment, after three days in the slime and the stink, when he saw the light and land and water, and knew the face of God?[2]

The experience of helplessness delivers us

directly to the sacred. The face of God, the opening of the gate — we know what it is after having seen this, whether we use these terms or find other words to convey the gravity of the experience. We are blessed with enough fear to see the world anew. The challenge is to let what we have glimpsed mark the rest of our lives, to remember what mattered to us then and what did not, rather than to slip right back into unknowing as soon as we are able to resume our regular doings.

Power, money, individual aspiration — these are not in the forefront when we are facing death. A heart muscle that could cease pumping at any moment, or a tumor threatening to obstruct a vital function brings us face to face with all that is transcendent. Our relationships shine with primacy, becoming the sun in which we warm ourselves and from which we derive the strength to bear whatever transpires.

When whales are cut loose from entanglement in fishing lines, the divers in most intimate contact invariably recount a life-changing encounter. They sound much like those who return from a near-death experience, describing an all-encompassing sense of peace. A diver who freed a humpback whale from crab-trap lines near the Farallon Islands said, "When I was cutting the line going through the mouth, its eye was there winking at me, watching me. It was an epic moment of my life." After the whale was freed, it nuzzled him and each of the other rescuers before swimming off.[3]

I once asked a particularly warmhearted oncologist how he could stand to have so many of his patients die, yet remain so open in his relationships. He revealed that every year he goes into remote areas of Alaska where grizzly bears preside, armed with only a camera. "If a hungry bear finds me out there, the simple fact is that I am lower on the food chain. Each time, I have to get through being afraid. Something comes over me — a sort of recognition — and then I'm good for another year."

Each of us must come to acceptance of mortality on our own. There is no difference between this doctor's exposure to death in the woods and that which threatens his patients. He does all he can for them, but it is in the nature of things that a bear or a tumor will take a life from time to time. Finding peace in the beauty of the world and the workings of nature includes participation in the rhythms of living and then dying.

In the Yom Kippur liturgy, there is a passage that is jarring and comforting in equal measure: "O Lord, before I was formed I had no worth, and now that I have been formed, I am as though I had not been formed. Dust am I in my life; yea, even more so in my death."[4] To be shaken up to this degree, whether in a hospital, a synagogue, or an ocean, is the heart of spiritual reckoning. It is what we are seeking, beyond human endeavors, when we wish to be touched by the sacred.

As we get older, spiritual needs pull at us like a rising tide. Our interest in the sacred increases as loved ones die and our attachment to the material world fades. The fundamental questions about life become less abstract. We find that the value of private attainment wanes in comparison to seeing ourselves as part of a transcendent story. Our yearning for something overarching like the divine to explain what is going on is never greater. The profane loses its sway with us as we seek to become conversant with larger truths.

When Barbara Myerhoff, the anthropologist, was dying at the age of forty-nine, she participated in healing rituals with a Hasidic community. In a film documenting her discoveries at this juncture, she sits casually on a couch, gaunt from her illness, and observes: "These people have the fundamental human heritage that the rest of us have lost — spirituality and community." She had been especially impressed by the purification ritual of the *mikvah,* an immersion in water common to religious practices all over the world. "It was in a way mine all along. It was what I belonged to without knowing it. And I suppose that's a treasure, really, that they've given me."[5]

7
Generosity

Ultimately, you cannot save yourself
without saving others. Other-preservation
is the first law of life.

MARTIN LUTHER KING JR.

We are fortunate when aging extricates us
from an excessive focus on ourselves. More
than anything else, losses in later life can
awaken our sympathy and make us stay attuned to the importance of living in concert
with others. An interest in serving broader
aims may keep mounting — contributing to
our local community, helping to ensure the
health of natural areas in our vicinity —
whatever we can do that connects us to the
human prospect as a whole, even in a small
way.

Most of us become convinced that the
spirit for a life well lived derives from what
we give to others, not from what we amass
for ourselves. During times when we have

little influence over painful events in our own lives, we may still be encouraged by the effect we are able to have on others' circumstances. No matter what happens, we know that we can always do something for someone else.

Antonio Luis Alves de Souza, a Brazilian drummer, was offered an expensive new car after his band recorded *The Rhythm of the Saints.* Paul Simon wanted to thank him for the excellence of his artistry, beyond what he had already been paid. Instead, Souza requested money enough to buy an old building where he could teach theater arts, singing, and dancing to poor children and women from the streets. Fifteen years later, when he died of a heart attack at the age of fifty-four, his funeral procession "was followed by 4,000 people dancing and singing his songs."[1]

In a café one afternoon, I overheard the wrap-up of a business meeting between a woman in her fifties and a man in his thirties. She said, "So, I really like where we're going with this. I want to do something good for our community." The younger man replied, "That's great. I want to get paid." They were clearly at divergent points in the life course, with different priorities. After an awkward pause, they parted politely.

We naturally get caught up in making our way in the world during youth and middle age. There is little time or energy for endeavors beyond our personal sphere — maintaining a home, going to work, raising children. Two or three decades may elapse before we find these involvements less consuming. In the meantime, a longing for connection to something beyond these spheres slowly gains force.

Later life is the time when we tend to have room in our lives for generosity. It gives us reasons to prevail over our personal difficulties and grants us access to vital sources of renewal. We find there is strength in doing what good we can for others, not as an intellectual construct but as a robust way of meeting each day.

A newly retired county executive was rattled when no one called him anymore. His list of calls to return, previously pages long, had vanished altogether. The younger man who replaced him at the office had politely declined his offer of a lunch date, claiming he was mastering the job "just fine." This 68-year-old man was the same person he had been six months earlier but, without the trappings of his position, no one sought him out. He despaired: "I feel as though I have ceased to exist."

Playing golf more often did not help. A friend pestered him to take on a volunteer job, pointing out that he seemed to be getting more and more depressed. He admitted that he had been sleeping in later and later, sometimes not getting dressed until the afternoon. He began serving as a crossing guard for the elementary school just a few blocks from his house, figuring this would at least get his day started.

Right away, he noticed an overweight, awkward boy who was shunned by the other kids. He made a point of chatting with the boy, and soon he was letting him handle the flag each morning. The boy became his enthusiastic deputy. Adept at signaling the oncoming cars and getting them to halt yards before the white lines, he took on a straighter posture and a more confident gaze.

Prior to retiring, this man had not been one to ever consider how a man with a flag could become a source of hope to a scorned child: "I'd see these old guys with their orange vests and think how pathetic to have nothing else to do but get kids across the street. See, I was hot stuff with my fancy suits and my big car and more than fifty employees answering to me. Then — puff

— it was all gone. Just like that, I was nobody."

Removed from what he thought his life was all about, he was able to step across the barrier of his self-designated superiority. Then he found a more compelling reason to get out of bed in the morning. A few months into his new life, he remarked, "Just the idea of seeing this kid gets me going, even in the rain. I have never felt so jazzed." What had seemed utterly humble was now resonating with significance. It was crucial for him to show up each morning to praise his deputy. Nothing in his former job had mattered quite like this.

Generosity calls us to life. Involvement in the lives of others is ever replenishing, while pining for self-fulfillment drains the spirit. Searching constantly to find something more for ourselves leads to a deadening loop. We are lucky when circumstances force us to focus on something outside ourselves, or when we have the chance to give to someone what we are able to offer.

An 84-year-old woman living alone, facing considerable limitations from chronic pain, had her afternoons remade every few days by a knock on her door. The 12-year-old boy from a few houses down would appear, clutching a sheaf of papers. His mother was overwhelmed with side effects from the chemotherapy that was keeping her aggressive cancer at bay and could no longer help him with his homework. He would be there to show her what he had accomplished since their last session of editing and feedback on his writing assignments.

For both the boy and the woman, their time together at her kitchen table was a taste of peace, a chance to focus their minds on their skill with words rather than on cancer or pain. A plate full of freshly made chocolate chip cookies usually accompanied their labors. She knew that he got to be a boy again for an hour or so, rather than a son desperately worried about his mother. He told her that he could concentrate at her house in a way that he could not at home. She found that her shoulder pain often vanished entirely as she stirred the cookie dough and chased after misplaced commas.

There is nothing like finding our way back to true usefulness. Pain tends to fill the space left without other involvements, while engagement in other spheres of life crowds out a focus on maladies. As soon as she would hear his knock at her door, her pain would begin to subside. Sometimes just picturing him at her kitchen table gave her a whiff of relief, even on a day when she was not expecting him. The days without him tended to be long and empty, with the ache of her shoulder commanding her hours and thrusting her back into unwelcome self-pity.

Paying attention to other people takes us out of ourselves in the most relieving ways. While self-interested pursuits tend to exhaust us over time, contributions to the lives of others tie us into reliable sources of energy. When we know we are making a difference in someone else's life, the body's humiliations matter much less.

A high-powered CEO retired at the age of sixty due to restlessness. Still in good health, he had enough money to go anywhere and do anything he wanted. He decided to put out the word that he was available to any nonprofit CEO in his town who wanted help managing budgets in a tight economy. Within a few months, he had a long waiting list. Younger associates at his former company prodded him to turn this free tutoring into a lucrative consultancy. Over and over again, he had to explain that he was doing exactly what he wanted to do — that it was a privilege not to have to charge for his services. They were baffled, wondering if something was wrong.

The truth was that something was entirely right. The tutoring had quickly become one of his proudest achievements. "Before, each and every hour at work had to be cost-effective. Now I concentrate on seeing people grow. It's electric. My mentees really trust me. They know I have no motivation besides their success." By putting his mentees' well-being and development before any other concern, he was spurring his own renaissance. "I just wish I had more hours in the day."

Interest in others is one of the most attractive qualities in a person of any age. Elders who convey eagerness toward getting to know younger people and learning something from them tend to be the most venerated. There is a sense of discovery when in dialogue with such individuals, as compared to those who give in to a predictable recitation of ailments and complaints about their circumstances.

When she was nearing ninety, the writer Diana Athill described how being in contact with children and youth serves as a reminder:

[W]e are not just dots at the end of thin black lines projecting into nothingness, but are parts of the broad, many-colored river teeming with beginnings, ripenings, decayings, new beginnings — are still parts of it, and our dying will be part of it just as these children's being young is, so while we still have the equipment to see this, let us not waste our time grizzling.[2]

A 66-year-old surgeon who had been long accustomed to leading teams in the operating room recalled how ardently he had always argued for his point of view. His need to be right would trump the feelings of others, and he often found himself investing considerable energy in disputes. At his current stage in life, however, he was surprised at how ready he was to let his opinion slide. "I say what I have to say, and I let it go. It's useful to the other person or it's not. This is quite a change for me."

Our conversations change as we look for chances to foster others rather than seek our own benefit. A different kind of dialogue ensues when we do more listening than professing. Once we reach the point where we have won enough arguments or outshined enough colleagues, there is little need to vie for prominence. We have already satisfied the question of our own worthiness. We are not distracted by rehearsing a rebuttal or fashioning a counterargument to demonstrate our erudition. Instead, we are more likely to notice someone else's need to be affirmed and feel happy to supply the boost.

This surgeon found that guiding young doctors had become much easier and more interesting than ever before. With no need to demonstrate the superiority of his skill, he could sit back and wait for optimally receptive moments. "Younger people generally want to articulate their own ideas, rather than hear from an old workhorse like me. Sometimes they show me a thing or two. But then they reach a point where they do want to know what I know, and I'm happy to provide it."

The rewards for this transformation are ample. Inspiration flows most abundantly in two directions at once, as the heft of long experience meets the freshness of inexperience. Graced by fellow feeling, the responses pick up steam. Finding common ground in another becomes the basis of exciting interchanges, along with divergences that spark debate. In the best of circumstances, the roles of teacher and student — giver and receiver — move back and forth in a mutually welcome and creative flux.

Many of us find it increasingly necessary

to play a contributory role in others' lives and to see them do well. This is the embodiment of what the psychologist Erik Erikson called *generativity,* the culminating stage of our development.[3] Putting our hard-won competence to use vindicates the effort that went into acquiring what we know. If we follow these yearnings and use the bounty from our life's work on behalf of others, we gain the sweet sensation of power well employed. Furthering others' lives may become the primary motivation of our days and the source of consummate strength as we face the further challenges of getting older.

When she was nearing sixty, a motivational speaker with a national following began handing over some of her choice work to younger colleagues:

It's not that my time has passed or that I don't want to do it anymore. I have a lot to do yet. But it seems O.K. now to let younger people take center stage. It gives me a kick, actually, to see someone's name on the program at a major conference and know I helped get her there. I feel like this is what I should be doing with my life right now — promoting, mentoring those who are starting out. This is what turns me on.

When I started working in a nursing home, I was told about a 91-year-old resident everyone referred to as "The Angel." She had few visitors from the outside world, having never had children and having outlived most of her friends and relatives, yet she was rarely alone. The staff on her unit fought over being assigned to take care of her, and some of the nursing assistants from other floors would drop in to see her when they went off their shifts. I decided I had to find out the secret of her popularity in a place where most forms of personal influence drain away.

Her magnetism was clear within a few minutes of being in her room. Somehow she got me talking about my love for walking in the woods and the places in the world I have most enjoyed hiking. "You don't tell your stories to her," one staff member remarked. "You find out what your stories are." Her curiosity spurred me on to tangents in all directions. I lost track of time and almost missed my bus home that day. I looked forward to seeing her again, like everyone else, and eventually made a ritual of stopping in to see her during my break times.

The warmth of her presence and the eagerness of her interest always left me refreshed.

8
GIVING AND RECEIVING

Interdependence is the truth of our lives.
MAGGIE KUHN

Throughout our lives, we know that we need each other — especially during times of sickness and grieving — but in our youth we can keep our recognition of this reality at bay. It is often possible to maintain the myth of independence long into midlife, holing up in a private residence and feeling secure in our ability to fend for ourselves. The myth implodes as soon as someone close to us becomes incapacitated.

More than anything else, becoming a caregiver places us in a situation of accelerated awareness of our interdependence. A 44-year-old woman taking care of her 70-year-old mother-in-law experienced a period of rapid change as a result of devoting herself to this commitment:

One of the greatest benefits is developing relationships and giving up old ways of controlling. Accepting another person's reality works with all people in my life. . . . Caregiving has taught me that we are responsible to, not for, each other and that relationships are not disposable. It has allowed me to grow in ways that, without it, I don't think I would have grown.[1]

Witnessing a loved one's transition from autonomy into dependence forces us to ponder all of our relationships. *Who would take care of me if I became frail?* This question moves us beyond wondering to a serious concern. We know that accepting help someday will not be easy. We might be exposed to the universe of vulnerability, on the side of those who must receive.

As we consider our ultimate need for it, kindness rises in our esteem. We begin noticing true communities, contexts where a fine character, faithfulness, and decent conduct matter a great deal. Our respect for the workings of reciprocity heightens. In thinking about who would come through for us, we realize more than ever that the quality of our relationships is the basis for hope. A 66-year-old woman observed, "You live out of ego-striving, until a reflection gets going. Then you let go of all that and move into a more interdependent, co-created kind of reality. I don't know how else to describe it, but it is a powerful shift in consciousness."

In a city neighborhood not too far from the White House, a group of elders banded together to organize Capitol Hill Village. The idea was to foster a system of exchange in which needs would be matched with abilities across generations, resulting in a means for elders to remain in their own homes. A retired seamstress in her eighties might be connected to a businessman in his thirties who occasionally needs someone to hem his slacks. He might be happy to mow an older person's patch of lawn on Saturdays or run errands for a homebound elder.

In the beginning of the project, the founders worried that there would be a shortage of younger volunteers and a surplus of elders hoping to get some help. To their delight, they ended up with more people wanting to give than receive. Their list of services offered just kept on growing. Harriet Rogers, one of the elders who was a charter member, attested to the pleasure of both giving and receiving: "Volunteering has been as rewarding as membership. I'm glad to be plugged in. . . . I have made new friends for the first time in a long time."[2]

This impulse toward mutual aid is consistent with our biology, our spirituality, and the truth of our need for each other. Communities cohere around this foundation. The anthropologist Barbara Myerhoff termed such cooperative alliances "networks of reciprocity,"[3] with each person aware that what is given today might be received tomorrow. It turns out that individuals of all ages are glad for opportunities to give to one another, increasing their certainty that they will be able to count on kindness during their time of need. Reciprocity is the moral center of both the idea and the practice of community.

When such exchanges are intergenerational and occur within the normal course of living, neither the old nor the young need be ashamed of depending on each other. Help can be accepted without forfeiting dignity. The community itself becomes the commons, and there is confidence that everyone will contribute their share. Elders are valued as younger people are naturally drawn to learn about life from those who have already proven themselves. Everyone does better as a consequence of generations relying on one another. Recognizing our lifelong interdependence allows us to give help with a sense of the inherent privilege of doing so.

I once knew a woman in her early seventies who required two hours to get dressed every morning due to terrible pain in her hands: "I refuse to feel sorry for myself. I won't go down that road. Too many people are counting on me." She had several neighbors in their nineties who could not get their groceries or other necessities without her. These were the elders of her youth, the parents of friends who had long since moved away. When she had returned to the neighborhood to take care of her own parents years before, they had assisted her with errands and everything else. It gave her great comfort to repay them, no matter how much her hands ached.

In Yellowstone National Park, I got lost one night trying to find my way back to our campsite from the restroom. I had forgotten my flashlight, and the darkness was bewildering and deep on the return trip. The longer I searched for our tent, the more confused I became. The only beacon in the distance was a campfire that had been lit by one of the campground hosts. It was the last night of the summer season, and she laughed genially about having helped many others in my predicament.

She explained that the next day she and her husband were packing up their mobile home and traveling around for a few more months before winter set in. As the campfire crackled in front of us, she described missing her friends and her small town ever since she and her husband had begun their nomadic life when he turned sixty-five. It had been six years already:

> Winters, we park by each of our kids' homes for two months at a time. That takes care of six months, and we get to see our grandchildren. Then in the spring we travel around for a few months, going to places we've never been, and each summer we are hosts at a campground somewhere pretty. My husband says we should feel at home in ourselves, but I feel homeless. I especially feel it on nights like this, when we are about to pull up our stakes and move on. I feel like a vagabond. Not the romantic kind. The lonely kind.

In my youth, I had seen older couples in their motorized monoliths and presumed their freedom was exhilarating. But since then I have learned there is always a duality in freedom. Such couples can certainly go wherever they want to go, but often at the cost of experiencing an underlying disquietude. Not belonging to a community means not being linked to others by an ongoing exchange. If we are obliged to no one else, we must create the content of our lives afresh, day after day. Little holds the months together when our days begin and end only with ourselves. Embarking on one journey after another, we may find that our lives fall into a directionless drift.

Many who retire with ample financial resources believe that almost perpetual travel is the answer to the question of what to do with the rest of their lives. Giving up their homes, they end up with a list of exotic destinations attained and a pile of photograph albums or digital archives to which others grant polite attention. Alternatively, older couples who go on adventures yet return to deeply rooted communities for most of the year seem to do much better, retaining an active place in the lives of others.

Our relationships are our grounding, more than our mementos. Commitments propel us forward with the momentum of engagement. A history of having come through for others during their time of need becomes the basis for our security during times of loss and gives us the energy of solace when we need it the most.

I urged her to speak up, to tell her husband this was not the kind of life that filled her heart. I affirmed that being intertwined in the lives of other people is an advantage to be cultivated, not an encumbrance to be shed. She led me back to my campsite with her lantern, and I hope I prompted her to take a few steps back toward her community.

When I was in Nepal, I visited a family in a village three hours' walk from the nearest road. Electricity had not yet reached there, and water was hauled by bucket from the village well. As I approached the house, I saw the grandmother minding a toddler and the grandfather tending a horse. Their son, who had accompanied me there, explained that his wife was off gathering firewood. This snapshot of a moment in the life of a family remains imprinted in my mind with special vividness.

It was as if I had gone back in time that morning. When a household is intergenerational and the economy is agrarian, everyone's hands remain busy contributing to the work of life. Elders are heeded as transmitters of vital knowledge about survival, and help is provided on all sides as part of an ongoing exchange. Having something to give in return — this is the essence of dignity.

Affluence brings ironic losses. For the majority of Americans, life is generally organized around our jobs. We often pick up and move according to the dictates of employment. This means many of us no longer live near extended family members and are unaccustomed to assisting one another on a daily basis. It is no wonder that we fear being regarded as a burden if we have to resume proximity to loved ones solely for the sake of being helped in our old age.

The need to exchange comfort and strength has impelled human beings to huddle together since the beginning of history. Solitary coping, no matter how determined, cannot compare with the embrace of a community to which we have contributed on an ongoing basis. Life feels far less precarious when we are bolstered by a history of reciprocity and a network of interdependent relationships.

A man who had a stroke in his late fifties recovered physically but remained altered by what he had seen during his period of duress:

It was an awakening, really. Before that, I never noticed people with walkers trying to hustle to get across the street before the light changed, or the ones who had trouble opening a heavy door while hanging on to a cane. I lived with my head down, minding my own business. Now, at the grocery store I'll spot a lady trying to reach a box of cereal on the top shelf and I'm right there getting it for her. It's a whole different consciousness. You can't tell by looking at me that I had a stroke, except for maybe a slight limp when I get tired, but I'm not the same person.

The vessel that carries our soul is fragile. Beginning to live in accordance with this awareness can mean a dramatic revision in one's way of life. This man and his wife started looking into co-housing and other intentional communities, seeking a living situation that would tie them to others' lives in practical ways. "I have this image of working side by side in a huge garden that feeds a dozen families," he explained. "Tending my own backyard plot just doesn't seem like enough to me anymore."

The luckiest people may be those who get a lesson in our ultimate interdependence and then recover. While they still have the capacity to contribute, they become determined to find and settle into a context where neighbors help one another, where people remember acts of generosity and are glad to assist in return. Some go back to places they lived long ago and pick up where they left off, departing from their individual strivings in the hope of gaining the more durable strength of loyalty.

Others launch this reorientation of their goals within their own families. "My kids are absorbing it all," a 46-year-old woman observed after her grandmother with Alzheimer's disease moved in.

Some of our friends think we are nuts, but I know we're doing the right thing. Children who have to share a room so that their great-grandma can live in the house learn a lesson about family loyalty. They hate how she keeps wandering into their room and messing with their things, but I sometimes catch them distracting her with stories and ushering her back to her own bed so patiently. You should see their faces when we put on music and she belts out a song, remembering all the verses and looking like the wonderful, strong woman who raised my mother and took delight in me all of my life. The light in her eyes comes back, and we all end up having a glow for the evening. I am making sure we have plenty of fun, and that some great memories get built in.

This woman felt privileged that she could afford to cut down to half-time work and that there was a day center nearby where her grandmother could be cared for while she was at her job. Even as they were grumbling, she was certain that her children were being quietly infused with hope for their eventual fate as elders. After I sat in their living room and watched her 9-year-old daughter picking out notes on the piano with her great-grandmother, I was certain that these experiences would become the kind of recollections that would later inspire her care for her parents.

At age fifty-one, Renee Weinhouse survived stage-four lymphoma. Ever since, she has been visiting cancer patients at Montefiore Medical Center in the Bronx. Now seventy-nine, she also runs survivor support groups. "Nothing makes me happier than when I give a patient a little hope."[4] The hope rebounds to her as energy to get on the subway and move through her own down-turns, aware of all the people awaiting her inspiration.

Life improves when we attend to our interdependence, whether we add to the available goodness or draw from it. It is fortunate, then, that a sharpened awareness of the needs of others accompanies the poignancy of our own humbling. Those who do not miss a chance to make life easier for someone else wake up each day with eager-ness and have less fear about their own future. The happiest elders I have seen are those actively involved in their communi-ties, coloring their lives with the vibrant hues of engagement. Confidence in the power of kindness becomes a beacon, like a campfire on a dark night.

■ ■ ■ ■

PART TWO:
TRANSFORMATION

■ ■ ■ ■

9
TIME

A wild patience has taken me this far.

ADRIENNE RICH

The greatest divergence between young and old is how time is experienced. A year, that twelve-month mark of time's progression, is a fourth of a 4-year-old child's life but only one fortieth of what a person has experienced by the age of forty. The slices of time get slimmer. By the time we reach eighty, we do feel like we are having breakfast every fifteen minutes.

To study the subjective nature of time, scientists at the University of Rostock's Zoological Institute kept cattle ticks waiting for eighteen years before letting a mammal pass within their reach. Butyric acid in mammal sweat triggers the tick to leap off a branch, bury its head into a mammal's skin, and pump itself full of blood:

The tick represents, in the conduct of its life, a kind of apotheosis of subjective time perception. For a period as long as eighteen years nothing happens. The period passes as a single moment; but at any moment within this span of literally senseless existence, when the animal becomes aware of the scent of butyric acid, it is thrust into a perception of time.[1]

At will, I can arrest time and enter the same unfolding existence available to a child. I can choose to sit on my front porch with my 5-year-old granddaughter on my lap and feel her ease against me as we watch the sultry summer afternoon. We can listen to the woodpecker pounding on the metal box atop the utility pole, getting no insect lunch out of the metal but liking the drama of the sound. In this regard, how much time I have left to live is up to me.

There is little that is objective about time, beyond the numbers on a clock. The degree of expansion or contraction of the available moments is as personal as it gets. I can decide to befriend the approach of death as a reminder to live well, or I can throw away whole afternoons with fruitless anxiety. Just as surely as death imposes brevity, I must bestow worth.

I have been keeping a journal, unbroken, since fifth grade. In adolescence, I stopped calling it a diary and cast aside the kind with a fake leather cover and a tiny lock. Now it is covered with Italian marbled paper and I write with fine pens on an archival-quality surface. The style of my entries has also changed, but the enterprise of jotting down what I make of my days is essentially the same. I ask myself what is worth remembering, and the act of writing it down gives me the assurance that it will not be swept away in the rush of days going by.

Somewhere along the line, the practice of recording my days became necessary to me. I cannot go for long without opening up my journal and capturing what has been going on in my life. My tolerance for getting behind is about ten days, and then I become desperate to catch up and get something of those days inscribed. If it was once a discipline, now it is part of how I live.

When I get overloaded in a race with time, I retain little of the profusion of events. At night, our brains prune back much of what took place; there are limits to what can be stored and retrieved cerebrally. With delay, my journal entries become skimpy and superficial. To make my days deserving of preservation, I have to give myself ample time for reflection and repose. I need to have my pen in hand, the blank page in front of me, with the ticking clock as a companion in immediacy rather than as a taskmaster.

It feels as if such entries add an extra layer to living. Chronology becomes remembrance, day after day, as moments and conversations that would have been lost to time are fixed on the page, indelible. I accept my own impermanence, but I cannot stand to lose a week or a month. When I reread an old journal, time and memory collapse into each other in a way that makes the past come vividly into the present. I know I am cheating forgetfulness, not death.

The capacity to pause, to deliberately step back and consider our words and actions, is a skill to be cultivated. In youth, impatience often rules us. It is satisfying to spew out our reactions. Putting aside what feels good right now for the sake of the future smacks of stodgy merit, something recommended by the anxious or the old. Later, we incur the toll for imprudence, for blurting out our thoughts when we should have weighed what we wanted to say, or acting in haste when it would have been better to bide our time. We gradually see the benefits of learning how to wait.

A woman who grew up in a violent family spent her twenties and most of her thirties buffeted by the anger that surged with the slightest affront. She lost jobs and relationships over and over with her outbursts. In her late thirties, she started taking note of hurt as it arose and was astonished at her wild sensitivity. A catch in someone's voice, a subtle hardening in someone's eyes — she was alert to the most subtle of nuances. This radar had helped her survive earlier on, but it was time to recalibrate her sensitivity.

When her boss next made her furious, she excused herself and hurried to the restroom in order to shake off her rage. Locked safely in a stall, she prayed, breathed deeply, and imagined the day when she could walk away from the job. She was able to gather herself and let her feelings settle down. On subsequent occasions, she used the mirror to provoke further self-awareness, splashing cold water on her face until her fierce expression softened. Slowly, she gained mastery of her reactions, even though she often had to pretend to have an illness requiring urgent departures from her desk.

With intimates, she learned to ask for a time-out when her barometer of hurt and anger threatened to rise beyond reason. She took brisk walks around the neighborhood by herself, long retreats to the bathroom, or pulled over to the side of the road when an eruption threatened in the car. With friends, she would remind herself that a call not returned could mean the person was overwhelmed and was probably not rejecting her. She had to be on guard about negative assumptions, and instead ask questions. Each time she perceived a downturn in a friend's demeanor, she would tell herself that it was unlikely that the shift in mood had anything to do with her.

To be ruled by first reactions constricts a person's life in ways that become most apparent as soon as a measure of control is gained. Suddenly, feedback comes rushing in. The person sees how others have been careful, lest they set off a barrage of accusations, and have been afraid to be forthcoming with their own needs. The honesty is like fresh air in a chamber that had been too long sealed. No longer threatened by speaking the truth, everyone breathes easier and relationships start feeling more spacious.

Eventually, this woman was able to choose to remain silent when she felt tumultuous emotions rising up. She no longer lived at the mercy of her own temper. Her tenure in jobs and relationships lengthened dramatically. The occasions when she had to exert considerable effort to retain her self-control occurred less and less often. She had gained the freedom to employ the best possible combination of her heart and mind.

When our marriage went on the rocks shortly after our honeymoon, Barry and I met twice weekly with a couples counselor. During this period, my mother-in-law visited us and got a firsthand glimpse of our mutual misery. "Don't worry," she said, pulling me aside. "In two years he'll trust you."

Two years! I was young enough to find this idea outrageous. I thought she was kidding, but then realized that she was pleading for my forbearance. Forty years older, she saw two years as a reasonable interlude preceding what would surely be decades of union with a fine man. Now I am old enough to look back at my indignation and laugh. She was completely accurate, both in her estimation of the rate of trust's accrual and the fact that this was a small price for the balance of a good life with each other.

Learning how to wait is fundamental to living well; it is an alliance with the passage of time. Lifelong, tolerating delay requires certain basic strategies — expending effort, telling ourselves that things will get better, and making sure not to lose sight of the desired objective. Otherwise, we may fall out of practice with patience and abandon relationships or undertakings too soon. We must become adept at visualizing the reward while hungering for it, assuring ourselves all the while that it will be worth the wait.

As we get older, we tend to mull things over and defer at least some of our gratifications. We are better able to sit with our dilemmas, taking the time to air them with others rather than acting on impulse. We recognize that a difficulty might even prove to be a stepping-stone to something better than we can presently envision. More and more, we may be able to picture the aftermath of a predicament while we are still caught in it, as if we are already looking back at ourselves from a time to come when the current situation will not matter so much.

Our relationship with time is increasingly elastic; the past and the future are constantly in flux. Pauline Thompson, a 94-year-old Jungian psychotherapist, observed how her sense of impending discovery grew with the length of her past:

I'm realizing more aspects of the future in the last four years than I did in the other almost ninety. At one time I read a definition of old age as being "the sad process of going down a corridor watching the doors close as you go forward." But my experience has been that my old age has been an opportunity to see myself going toward the light with doors opening on both sides of the corridor as I go forward. My past accumulates up to now, and the farther back and outward it becomes conscious, the farther ahead I can extrapolate.[2]

We come to rely on time elapsing and bestowing its benefits. Trust is accorded through a long span of reliability and honesty, just as a good name is acquired through years of treating people decently and keeping one's word. Faithfulness earns the loyalty of friends, persistence develops our endurance, and confidence accrues with experience. Eventually, we get so much better at patience that we barely notice its slow virtue.

When I was in third grade, the teacher asked us to write down what our fathers did for a living on a piece of paper being passed around the classroom. The girl sitting next to me wrote DECEASED, and held the paper out to me. I had trouble extending my hand to take it, so frightened was I by that word — that such a word could be written about a daddy and by someone who was my age.

Some learn about death earlier than others, and this sets them apart. Such people do not necessarily show a bleak face to the world. Rather, they take what they grasp about life with them into happier occasions, quietly aware of what can be torn away from them at any moment. Their consciousness of transience accompanies them in everything they do and wherever they go for the rest of their lives.

At sixty-two, Harvard professor Sara Lawrence-Lightfoot proposed that a key challenge in later life "is figuring out how to navigate this tension between slowing down and speeding up, between mining the privileges of a well-earned patience and responding to the imperatives of time racing by."[3] Time, and life itself, have meaning only because of the provocation of death. We need both our finitude and our awareness of getting older, not just as reminders of time's value but as touchstones for living well.

10
HINDSIGHT

The afternoon knows what the morning
never suspected.

SWEDISH PROVERB

Chief among our gleanings from getting
older is newfound sympathy for the life
experience of others. Having gone through
hard times ourselves, we look at other
people's predicaments differently. A surge
of retrospective understanding may result, if
we apply what we have learned to our own
history. A friend reported that at age sixty-
five she was finally able to encompass the
point of view of those who hurt her long
ago:

My mistakes, my blind spots — I can think
about these now without shirking them. I
can see how frustrating I used to be for
people who loved me. Until now, it was
just too painful for me to peek into those

crevices of myself, to see what was there. It's not so hard now, not so humiliating. I'm so much less angry. I'm more tolerant of other people's dark sides, and this softens me toward myself as well. I'm so much less judgmental. I can see what we all struggle with. Where before I saw villains, now I see people doing their best with what they knew at the time, just like I'm trying to do.

Putting aside our own standpoint, placing another person's woe at the center of the story, can have reverberations throughout our lives. This added level of awareness may enable us to comprehend other people's ignorance or seeming insensitivity. Things that once seemed unforgivable can begin to make sense. We may see how it happened that a friend overlooked us during a time of need or why a parent spoke harshly and made things worse for us. The less severely we judge others, the more we may be able to ease up on ourselves. The breadth of new perspectives can give us a kind of second sight.

When she turned forty-five, a woman re-examined one of the key stories from her youth. Her father had lost his job when she was in her second year at a private college. He forced her to transfer to a state university when he could no longer afford the more expensive private tuition payments. It seemed he could have taken out loans or sought help from relatives, instead of disrupting her life so completely. For years, she told the story of being torn away from friendships by her insensitive father. The theme of having been cheated dominated her self-conception and her view of her family background.

Then, about twenty-five years later, her husband lost his job and they had to disrupt their children's lives by moving to another state where he could find employment in his field. As she fretted over the effects of the move on her children, she suddenly realized how much heartbreak her own father had endured, how he must have agonized each time he encountered the resentment she had wrapped around herself. She saw the many ways he had tried to make it up to her over the years, and how she had kept shutting him out.

Her view of her youth was altered fundamentally when she removed her shroud of bitterness, as was her whole life story:

So many things changed. I stopped finding hurt under every rock. I wasn't seeing unfairness everywhere I looked anymore. I saw a young woman who had to switch colleges, but who was so lucky she got to finish her degree. I saw a good father who did all he could, who used every resource he had to make that possible for his daughter. I just wish I could have seen this sooner and spared him all the hurt I put him through.

We are lucky if our parents are still alive when we get old enough to appreciate them. By extending our sympathy far beyond its earlier boundaries, we can try to inhabit their predicaments in our imagination. What we were only able to see from the outside so long ago bears little relation to what we can see years later, with the depth and complexity of having lived through our own difficulties.

A few months later, she flew back to her hometown and got to thank her father for having made sure there was enough money for her to finish her bachelor's degree. She told him she admired how he and her mother had managed to provide stability in the family, in spite of the financial upheaval. She cried as she apologized for how she had punished him for something that was out of his control, and he was tearful with the happiness of having won back his daughter's respect. "It's the same life," she said, "but now I tell a completely different story."

Linda Waterfall, the singer and songwriter, spent much of her youth trying to overcome the hurt her father caused her by discouraging her from making a career in music. When she was sixteen, he told her, "There's no use in doing that unless you're a genius. You're not a genius, and so you should pursue something more practical." She lost all confidence in herself. It was years before she was able to find her way back to her true desire: "My need for approval caused me to chase after things that really didn't nurture me. . . . I ended up getting lost periodically. It was like chasing a mirage in the desert."

While enduring poverty in order to focus on her music, she began to see why her father had traded his passion for playing clarinet for the duty of earning a living. He studied electronics and ended up working for Hewlett-Packard for most of his life. The older she got, the more she could visualize how hard it had been for her father to give up his own musical career in order to support a wife and two daughters. Then she went through cancer treatment and entered the emptiness of not knowing what was ahead for her. "That's when I got the courage to be able to face down the fears my dad had planted in me. . . . Finding the source of water inside yourself is really the answer." It was at this juncture that she moved into the most musically creative period of her life.

The routes to understanding are complex and often circuitous. We have to live long enough to have time for our stories to evolve. The passage of years often opens up layers of insight that we barely suspected earlier. We may see a great deal more about other people's motives and reactions, as well as our own responses. After many rounds of self-examination, we finally know which criticisms of ourselves to accept and which should be cast aside. We mull over the past once again, and this time we might find our way to revelation.

For her father's seventy-fifth birthday, just before he faded into Alzheimer's, Linda Waterfall was able to write him a card in which she told him he was her hero. She had needed to live the mirror image of her father's life in order to comprehend why he had admonished his vulnerable 16-year-old daughter so severely, and why he had even seemed jealous of her later musical success. To see her father's protectiveness where before she saw only his hurtfulness was a victory of life experience. In the grace of this clarity, she made peace with him and with herself.[1]

Hindsight tends to grow inside us as a nagging awareness before we grant it the status of knowledge. We all are distracted by our own obfuscations and evasions. We ascribe motive and intent to others on the basis of assumptions we mistake for facts. We may unwittingly live out our family themes for years, until something happens that jars us into seeing what has actually been going on. Then we have the opportunity to adjust our line of sight.

When we take another look, someone whom we once saw in a derogatory light may turn out to have been exemplary. A man in his early fifties was not able to see his father's full stature until many years after his death:

All along, I had very little respect for my dad. He just took it from my mom, time and time again. She could sure dish it out, and he wouldn't say a word. He would just wait for their fights to blow over, or try to calm her down if she was really out of control. Later on, when I was going through my divorce, the hassles were so intense that I thought of just packing up, leaving my kids, and moving to another state — just to be done with it all. Then I realized what my dad had done. He stuck it out for our sakes. In those days, he couldn't have gotten custody of us without a wicked court battle, so he stayed and paid the bills and kept her from going completely off her rocker. He was our quiet protector, for all of those years, when he could have cleared out and started over.

This man's father had given him a model of manliness that he was able to appreciate only when he faced his own quandary. He needed to draw on his father's example in order to figure out how to keep his self-respect while remaining faithful to his own children. Then he recognized an honorable sacrifice where before he had seen only demeaning capitulation. He decided to stand by his kids and fight for shared custody, all the while holding the memory of his father close.

There is always another side to the story, another layer beyond which the full impact has long been concealed. What we learn from our setbacks often illuminates aspects of earlier events to which we may have been oblivious at the time. Something from our own difficulties then startles us into a new way of seeing, reanimating the family sagas that had become leaden inside of us.

A woman of fifty had repeatedly gotten involved with charming men who drank heavily. When she forced herself to give less flashy men a try, boredom drove her back to those with outward polish and some kind of wild streak. Over and over again, a romance would flare brightly and then return her to the ashes of hurt and betrayal.

This woman's life could not get better until she admitted that she was caught in a pattern and faced its origins. In the desperation following her second divorce, she finally reflected upon having been raised by an alcoholic father whose attention she had sought in vain. She decided to confront the compulsion head-on by staying with the type of man she would have dumped before, a man who was trustworthy, loving, and not particularly exciting.

Going against her inclination was tricky at first. This meant putting herself through a succession of dull evenings watching movies on his living room couch or conversing in sedate restaurants, rather than dragging him around from one glitzy club to another. She was restless and ill at ease, often crabby, but his interest in what she had to say led her to quadrants of herself that she had never articulated before, to herself or anyone else. Eventually, she came to look forward to their many-layered conversations. This man turned out to possess the depth and devotion she had long craved. Her third marriage lasted for the rest of her life.

A 93-year-old woman often mulled over how her life would have turned out with the suitor she had rebuffed in preference for a more reliable fellow. She had remained amicably married to this calm and faithful man until his death at the age of eighty-eight. "So, you see, I never got to feel that fire again. I'm certain life with that wild man would have been full of heartbreak, but I can't help wondering — sometimes for whole afternoons."

Having given up a lover can mean a lifetime of wistfulness in quiet moments. This woman did not want her 70-year-old daughter to know about this lost passion, fearing she would be judged disloyal to her husband. "He was such a good father," she sighed, "just not the liveliest of men." Sworn to secrecy, I was treated to racy stories of everything forbidden in which she had indulged at the age of nineteen. "It was the Twenties, dear. So I wasn't the only one. Don't forget that."

11
Decisions

Joy and woe are woven fine.

WILLIAM BLAKE

It is not easy to figure out how to live. Youth is so burdensome because we have to decide which direction to take in many domains at once. Choices made in our twenties feel like the hinges upon which the rest of our lives will swing. We wonder if we are supposed to make our own fate, or if there is something distinctly ours waiting to be found that we could miss if we do not watch out for it. There is nothing we can do but carry the weight of it all.

A 66-year-old woman remarked, "The answers to lots of things that tormented me when I was younger have been resolved. Will I get married? Will I have kids? What kind of work will I do? It's all settled now. I would never want to be in my twenties again. I'll take the body, but I wouldn't want the life."

By the time we become elders, we have the benefit of every crossroad we have already passed. There have been hundreds of roads not taken. We worry much less about making a wrong choice, since some of our carefully considered decisions have led to dead ends and some of our gut impulses have led to unforeseen gains. We realize that the very idea of a wrong or right choice is falsely polarizing. No matter what decision we make, we know we may end up pining for some aspects of the life we declined even as we celebrate the many advantages of having moved on. No one does any better than this.

At the age of twenty-three, I faced a choice I found overwhelming. Out of the blue, a job offer came that meant I would have to break commitments I had made to two jobs and a boyfriend. I was working part-time as an aide in a psychiatric hospital in downtown Philadelphia, and had just gotten promoted to work with a team I respected a great deal. I was also tutoring inner-city high school students five nights a week in exchange for room and board. I loved living in the big, suburban house with these kids, giving them a better chance at succeeding in life than they could have gotten in their chaotic home neighborhoods.

I had forty-eight hours to decide if I wanted to serve as dean of the junior class at Wesleyan University in Connecticut. A dean had resigned just as the academic year was beginning, and they needed someone who knew the school well enough to take over immediately. I was first on the list of recent graduates they were planning to contact.

I was gyrating with indecision, unable to sleep or eat. Should I break my commitment to my team at the hospital? How could I disappoint the kids I had been tutoring for a year, who trusted me and with whom I had gotten so close? Was it a good idea to leave such a promising romantic relationship? I liked my new life in vibrant Philadelphia. Would returning to my college town be a move back ward, or forward? Which was the path I was supposed to follow?

I was lucky to be able to air my dilemma with an elder. With twenty-four hours left to decide, I took a long walk with one of the board members of the tutoring project who had offered his counsel. He was retired, in his late sixties, with intense eyes and a gentle manner. He heard me out. When I finished delineating all my elaborate permutations, he said, "Years from now, what will have been the right choice? As pained as you are to leave these relationships at work and with the kids, how could you not take this unusual opportunity? Think of how this juncture will seem in years hence."

I was startled by his certainty. I suddenly saw myself as an elder, looking back on this young woman who was too afraid of disappointing others to grab hold of what she really wanted to do. On that tree-lined street with its elegant houses and expansive lawns, I was young and I was old. I was also myself, and I saw that I should take the job. I suspected I would never regret it. I made the call to accept as soon as I returned to the house. Within a few days, I quit my hospital job, resigned from the tutoring project, broke up with my boyfriend, and packed up my belongings.

During my stint in the dean's office, I helped scores of confused students choose a major, wrestle with what to do with their lives, and bear the agonies of break-ups and conflicts with roommates. Exposure to so many life stories made me fluent in varieties of sympathy and gave me inklings of my future as a therapist. My self-confidence grew at a pace that my former life in Philadelphia could not have matched.

Viewing their lives from the outside, we might think that those we admire got to where they were through a sequence of well-made plans. Now that I am older, I know that almost everyone operates more by feel than by design. Most of us have only a vague idea of where we are going. At best, goals are guesses, not assured destinations. We may zigzag here and there, or circle back to the familiar before we break out of it and move ahead. Once we find our way, we devise a narrative that makes it sound as though we had made well-reasoned decisions that cohered all along. Now I can see how that board member from the tutoring project knew just what to say to me.

A professional musician in his late forties reached the point where he needed to try to make a living in some other way. He needed to let music go back to being a joy, rather than a taskmaster. He sought a shift in his aims that would animate his spirit, to see what might emerge if he disrupted the terms of his life: "I want to be knocked off course."

Choosing to heed the rumblings of discontent can be dangerous. Why interfere with a good enough life? We do not know where dissatisfaction will lead us, once we decide to respect our gut reactions and halt the evasions that allow us to avoid our own truth. We are not even sure that we would recognize fulfillment if we found it. There is only the process of feeling our way through the upheaval, opening ourselves to possibilities as we search out what comes next for us in life. Instead of seeking firm ground as soon as we can, we may need to endure a prolonged period of flailing.

This man had to impose on his wife's willingness to carry the family financially while he opened himself to exploration. Their children were still small, and household expenses were not going to pause. Quests of this kind often require difficult trade-offs, such as having less money in order to have more time, earning a smaller hourly wage but having a free mind at the end of the day for grappling with what is being awakened.

In a year's time, this musician moved from being a gardener at a fancy estate to a certified nursing assistant in a nursing home. There, he came face-to-face with challenges to his conception of himself. Doing shift work and earning just a little more than minimum wage, he had to fight feeling diminished. "Helping someone clean themselves up, there can't be even a whisper of disgust, of wishing you were someplace else.

I tell myself, this person is at your mercy. I have to make sure neither of us feels badly about what we are doing. Together, we keep our self-respect."

Each day that he refused to feel demeaned by the nature of his tasks, his spirit got stronger. The more he beheld the individuality of each person assigned to his care, the more he ennobled his work. He became more lighthearted, drawing out stories and good cheer from those who hungered for the dignity he made possible. "I am watching the work change me, bit by bit, and letting the realizations come as they will. I just need to keep listening to what is going on inside me."

Holding on to the necessity of listening, both inwardly and outwardly, was bringing him closer to clarity. He felt layers of expectations peeling off of him as he shed superfluous parts of himself. If youth is the piling on of identities out of a need to feel substantial, later life is boring down into the depths of the essential. He still did not know where he was heading, but he felt more certainty about the rightness of his quest.

The writer Frances Moore Lappé reached a similar point in her life when she could no longer bear to keep to the path she was on, yet she had no idea how to move forward: "I agonized so hard over my decision that I made myself sick. I couldn't move." Looking back on this juncture years later, she wrote:

> Walking into the unknown, whether a roomful of strangers, a dense forest on a cloudy night, or even a day without a plan, can be scary. . . . Yet we realize, too, that moving toward a life we choose requires letting go of the known, letting go of our story. Perhaps it means dropping labels we've relied on to tell us who we are, or giving up structures and paychecks we cling to. Perhaps it means feeling out of place with those we care about who can't fathom what we're up to. . . . In any case, it means saying, "I don't know." It means facing empty space and silence in a culture that equates stopping and silence with failure and indecision.[1]

By later life, we are no strangers to compromise. Our desires have been thwarted by reality's intrusions many times over. Ambivalence is not as uncomfortable as it once was, so accustomed have we become to conflicted feelings and contradictory attitudes. Long ago, we had to give up the search for absolute certainty, the imagined course of action that would yield all or nothing. As elders we are better able to tolerate muddling through, groping in the dark until we find our way.

A 61-year-old man ended up feeling victorious after a protracted period of resistance to making any changes for the sake of his health:

> My back was up against the wall. I had no choice, really. I had to quit smoking before my lungs gave out. But quitting gave me a terrific boost. While I was at it, I decided to go low fat, low carb, low salt. I'm a new man — the master of my mouth. I set my mind to it, and I did it. Then a lot of other things fell into place. I'm not on any prescription medicines anymore. I've lost thirty pounds, and I automatically walk three miles a day. My wife feels like a health nut has replaced her former husband.

Reaching the point where there is no other choice but to live differently can be a great boon. A looming disaster sometimes gets us scrambling like nothing else can. When things we once considered indispensable are taken away, we see how little we needed all along. By the time we reach the next upheaval, we may find we have become more nimble.

A 70-year-old man went straight from the hospital into a tiny apartment in an assisted-living residence. His daughter dispersed most of his belongings to friends, family, and charity, leaving him with one shelf of books. He told me that he was fine. "It was the big move I had always dreaded, and in one clean sweep it was done. The great thing was, I still had myself."

With aging we gain a stronger sense of inner continuity, making external shifts less consequential. So much persists underneath all our transitions that we are not easily rattled. Pressures may mount, especially if physical constraints worsen or financial limitations reduce our options, but our internal landscape tends to remain unfazed.

In later life, we have no further use for evasions. We prefer to go straight to the heart of the matter — what will be lost this time? We want to gather the facts and get on with the work of letting go. We only wonder how much disappointment there will be, not whether we will have to make adaptations. We know in the end there will also be the relief of moving forward and possibly some unexpected rewards.

"You make a decision and you don't look

back," announced an 89-year-old man recounting the day he gave up his car keys:

> I missed a stop sign. Just one stop sign. But the time had come to face it — my vision was getting worse and I was a hazard on the road. We're talking about my pride, my independence. Gone. Well, everything comes with gains and losses. My daughter started taking me grocery shopping once a week, and we've gotten much closer. We really talk now, not just chitchat. It's the best time I've had with her in years, and so this is the day of the week I look forward to the most.

When we try to retrace the steps that led to our taking one fork in the road of life rather than another, we may not be able to recall what tipped us toward the choice we made. Details of the circumstances that mattered so much to us at the time may have faded into inconsequence. The deciding factors could have been anywhere from wise to arbitrary, the distillation of alternatives pondered deeply or swayed by the toss of a coin. Alternatives come to us through a mix of complex factors, some of which we influence and others that arise from just plain luck. It is freeing in itself to see that we can take credit or blame for only a certain portion of what has befallen us.

I went on to marry someone else, as did the fellow I left behind in Philadelphia. More than twenty years later, we encountered each other in a hotel hallway at a professional conference. It was the break between sessions, and people were pushing past us as they headed off to the restrooms and coffee stands. We summarized the major events in our lives, all the while scrutinizing each other — a quick glimpse of the road not taken.

12
DETOURS

He who is aware of his folly is wise.

YIDDISH PROVERB

Life does not get better so long as we avoid the pain that spurs us to evolve. We do not develop emotionally, because we block out our feelings rather than bear them. We cannot become fluent in intimacy, because we keep ourselves hidden. We do not become confident, because we duck challenges rather than do the kind of work that instills self-worth. There are no shortcuts to life's bounty.

The most common path of avoidance is dependence on substances, but there are many ways to remain static. Any kind of evasion — working all the time, cutting ourselves off from emotion, immersing ourselves in incessant distractions — can deflect us from life's natural progression. We must move through difficulty, rather than try to get around it, if we wish to be strengthened by life experience.

To get back on track, we must let ourselves be instructed by our mistakes. Remorse becomes a spur to honor relationships to which we have granted insufficient respect. Wasted time calls us to make the most of our remaining years. Past deceptions demand a relentless dedication to honesty. When we are ready to push through the obstacles, even decades' worth, we can reach the good life waiting on the other side. Then life gets so much better.

Those who become involved in substances remain stuck at the age they were when they first began their habit. While their peers are gaining valuable skills by going through hard times and coming out the other side, they shirk opportunities to learn how to endure life's travails. Instead of transcending foul moods, they seek to control them. Rather than taking a brisk walk, talking to a friend, praying, listening to music, meditating, or gazing at the open sky, they dodge strain and stress by alleviating the burden chemically.

Dependence on substances may take hold in a life void of nurturing relationships, or plentiful devotion from others may be forfeited as a result of drinking and drugging. Either way, the relationship with the substance gradually becomes more central than any other tie, with loved ones an increasingly distant second.

Intimacy remains thwarted on all fronts as people in trouble with substances cordon off whole portions of themselves from scrutiny. They present a polished surface externally, a disguise that gives no inkling of the self-loathing concealed beneath. Some become charming and socially adept to an extreme degree. Their loneliness only grows more intense, the more skillful they become at hiding their interior reality.

Blaming everyone and everything but themselves, they must invent distorted versions of their life story in order to explain why things have not gone well for them. Children are harmed, marriages lost, parents alienated, jobs forfeited, and artistic talents squandered, yet people in trouble with substances still go on locating the origin of their misfortunes in the actions of others — rebellious children, selfish partners, critical parents, lousy bosses, a society unkind to artists. Their efforts at deflection convince no one but themselves.

Anyone who tries to point out the link between their substance use and their failures is likely to be met with wrath in response. Truth-speakers, no matter how loving and well-intentioned, tend to be dismissed as worriers and control freaks. In the meantime, the illness worsens and the damages add up. Denial of the harm caused by use of the substance becomes more intense. The focus on getting high becomes increasingly urgent as the harmful consequences keep piling up and the need for avoidance becomes more desperate.

There may be occasions when the mountain of harm becomes clearly visible to the addict. A terrible appraisal may occur, spurring an interest in change. The writer Carolyn Knapp explained that at her sickest point, nothing and no one mattered to her except drinking. One day while babysitting for her sister's children, she nearly lost her grip on the small child in her arms and came close to shattering the girl's skull on the pavement. This was the event that sent her into a treatment program.[1]

The impetus for reclaiming one's life and staying on course has to come from within. Feelings disregarded during the long period of denial must be taken out and experienced one by one — shame, grief, guilt, resentment, insecurity, anger, self-hatred, vulnerability, jealousy. The longer someone has been avoiding these emotions, the greater the backlog. No matter how vast the accumulation, the person has to remain diligent and truthful on every level while going through the process. Returning to the habit of evasion, even without actually using a substance, can instigate a relapse back into distorted ways of thinking that threaten what has been achieved. Recovery is a period of reckoning unlike any other.

Such transformation is available to us at any time. We can choose to acknowledge how we contribute to our own unhappiness, instead of making excuses and trying to shift responsibility onto others. A commitment to honesty and self-scrutiny puts us on track for a good life, no matter how long we have diverged from it.

Michael Geoghegan spent thirty-five years in jail for various crimes. His travails began at the age of nine when his father was sent to jail. His defeated mother then put him in a Catholic boys' home where he suffered extensive sexual abuse by a deacon. He participated in a string of bank robberies when he was twenty, which landed him in jail, and then later had his original sentence extended due to stabbing a guard.

While in prison, Geoghegan read thousands of books. He was particularly moved by Rilke's poetry. There was a juncture of despair when one of Rilke's poems helped him name his deepest woe:

> What will God do when I die? And I thought — nothing. You know, God would do nothing, because I don't exist in God's eyes. You know, I have no soul. It's been dead. And I always felt this vast emptiness inside of me. And it was only in the past fifteen years or so that I managed to learn that I do have the courage to heal.

When he left prison, Geoghegan could have locked himself up in bitterness, but he decided to turn himself into a person he could respect. His first act was to confront the church authorities. He wanted to make sure children presently served by the church did not have to suffer similar abuse. The current bishop heard him out and apologized for the church's wrongs. He also invited Geoghegan to assist the diocese in developing a program to help people coming out of prison, Faith Alliance Initiative for Transitional Healing (FAITH).

Creating something out of adversity is powerfully restorative. Geoghegan began altering the saga of his life by employing on behalf of others what he had learned through his ordeals. He found he knew exactly how to assist those facing the challenge of starting a new life against the odds. Years of reading in jail had given him words for the ache in his soul, as well as the capacity to comfort others. Advocating on behalf of other former prisoners, he made use of his suffering and filled his days with meaning. "The only goal I've really had since I got out of prison is to die with a good name."[2]

A woman in her late forties with a six-year sobriety began to isolate herself when her beloved father became seriously ill. Her best friend begged her to fight against this instinct and allow friends to surround her with support and affirmation. Instead, she reverted to her former pattern of living as though she were alone in the world. Then, when the illness overtook her father, she broke her sobriety and returned to the instant obliteration of pain that she had relied upon years before. After his funeral, she almost died in a weeklong binge and then lost her job when she returned to work hungover.

Her friend was frightened and angry in equal measure. It seemed as though her well-considered advice had been scorned and her loving support had been useless. She was still tempted to lend money, yearning to do something, but was aware that attempts at rescue would be fruitless. She knew that those who love someone dependent on drugs or alcohol must make sure that their lives do not decline in tandem with the person in trouble. She was aware that she had to protect herself from the consequences of her friend's addiction just as assiduously as her friend did not. Realizing it was best to keep her distance for a while, she took comfort in knowing that the six-year sobriety would serve as a source of hope as this surge of reckless self-destruction played itself out. Life skills mastered during the sober period would still be there when her friend was ready, as well as the AA community to which she had become attached.

Eleven months later, waking up one morning in bed with a man she did not recognize, the grieving woman was jolted into reclaiming her sobriety. Her recovery community welcomed her back with warmth and understanding, as did her friend. They resumed their relationship with gusto. In AA meetings and in self-reflection, she took on the demon of her bitter self-sufficiency for the first time. She was able to face the hurt she had absorbed in early childhood when her father had not yet become sober himself. Confronting these interlocking sources of bitterness and hurt, she was able to reach the first anniversary of her father's death more certain of her sobriety than ever. She dedicated her recovery to him.

Respect for ourselves and forgiveness of others derive from the same source — recognizing the universality of life's difficulties. It is calming to realize that much of what we contend with does not belong to us alone. This stance frees us to look honestly at resentments that had lodged in us long ago and to sympathize with others for having made their own mistakes. We thereby release ourselves and others at the same time.

It is possible at any point in life to heed the call of the finest aspects of our character. Many of us do not confront the fact that we are off course until our forties and fifties, and sometimes later than that. Whenever we are ready, we can decide to dedicate ourselves to coming out of hiding and grabbing hold of the challenges we have evaded. By opening ourselves to the full range of feelings, we can face what is behind our most difficult emotions. We can learn how to accept the vulnerability of our need for others and make ourselves available for loving and being loved. Lost time cannot be regained, but we can enter a period of rapid evolution.

In her early forties, the actor Jamie Lee Curtis entered a treatment program for her prescription drug and alcohol dependence. She then cut back her acting career in order to be there more fully for her children, and to pursue other interests such as photography, writing children's books, and serving as a spokesperson for children's charities. By the time she turned fifty, she was looking ahead at the rest of her life with clarity and strength. "I feel way better now than I did when I was twenty. I'm stronger, I'm smarter in every way, I'm so much less crazy than I was then. . . . Getting older means paring yourself down to an essential version of yourself."[3]

13
RESILIENCE

If your drink is bitter, turn it into wine.
RAINER MARIA RILKE

As we get older, we become increasingly confident that we will be able to bear whatever befalls us. We know that we can call upon capacities forged during past times of transition and trouble, employing every kind of creativity to get around obstacles. We become certain we can sustain ourselves through the well-practiced art of balancing losses with satisfactions, making things better by seeking out compensations. Over time, the misfortunes we endure hone our skills for living, then the alchemy of perseverance turns our struggles into strengths.

Gene Cohen, a physician and researcher, noted that "out-of-the-box thinking is a learned trait that improves with age." Over a long career, his research and clinical work demonstrated that getting older "allows our brains to accumulate a repertoire of strategies developed from a lifetime of experience."[1]

A 103-year-old woman who had been a single mom during the Depression recalled serving her sons dandelion greens and potato-peel soup. "Look, you can get used to anything if you put your mind to it. You get yourself up in the morning and just keep going, day after day. You tell yourself it will get easier, and it does." When she went blind in her early nineties, she devised a way to get dressed in the morning by feeling for zippers and buttons. When she could no longer read facial expressions, she learned how to get to know new people by memorizing their voices. "I know I'm a tough bird, but anyone can do it."

More essential than physical agility, mental resilience can be counted upon in all kinds of situations. A mind-set of pushing through hardship can be developed at any point and keeps expanding with use. A "masters-aged" athlete wrote:

> The older athletes I ride with are pretty tough. Like last Saturday, while the 20-somethings were snuggled in bed, sleep-

171

ing off the parties, we old guys were out there slogging away in the pouring rain. It wasn't fun, and that's the point. . . . I'll ride in the rain, ride alone and ride long. I'll ride with annoying people, through cities and in traffic. I'll ride when I'm hungover or even sick. Last Saturday, the rain was coming down and I put my head down and ignored the wet, the cold, the bad visibility. . . . I wasn't training my body as much as I was training my mind.[2]

When her husband of thirty years first left her, a woman in her mid-fifties could not envision that she would one day emerge from the darkness and outrage of the betrayal. Their married life had been placid. They were not unhappy. Somewhere along the way growth had ceased, but conflict was minimal. She was married for life and therefore could put up with compromises for the sake of this precious continuity. Then she was shattered.

When something happens that strips us down to our core, we see what we are made of — what remains when everything else is taken away. At first, she lingered in the abject state of having been rejected, cast off by someone in whom she had invested three decades of trust. The terms of her life had been broken, and she could not imagine what other basis there could be for living out the rest of her years. It was sheer anguish, worse than bereavement because it did not have to happen, and she did not see it coming clearly enough for any measure of preparation.

Gradually, this woman found her footing. She was able to feel the contours of her character and gifts of sensitivity. She took stock of her friendships, work relationships, and her bonds with her adult children, realizing that she was well regarded from all sides. Her husband had not walked off with her self-respect.

"Failure and loss don't gnaw at me so much," she remarked a year and a half later. "I'm beginning to move out into life without so many personal constrictions." She had entered a vital, exploratory phase unlike any she had ever experienced, feeling more malleable than she had been since childhood. She was mustering her talents, day by day, to see where they would lead, and slowly assembling strengths that had been lying in wait.

Once we become receptive to inner expansion, the progress inherent in living picks up speed. We are compelled to transcend the narrow path we have been on. We gain a more supple relationship with our memories as well as our expectations.

Each small advance brought her longer periods of peace. With life widening beyond her prior hopes, she was beginning to understand both why they had stayed together for so long and why it was better that their mutual confinement had ended. "I never thought I would feel grateful to him for abandoning me. But so many of the limits were self-imposed, and I couldn't see this until he wasn't there to blame." She was starting to make a comeback with poise and verve.

To get up a steep trail with a backpack, I have to proceed at the pace of an inchworm. My difficulty is mechanical: My diaphragm happens to be located high under my narrow rib cage, and thus my lungs cannot expand as fully as they might. I huff, puff, and repeat to myself, *One step at a time.* Since I have never known a further ease, I am not impatient. I know I will get there, that I only must persist. So it is with every striving that really matters to us.

With each successive year of living, we become more practiced at putting one foot in front of the other in the steady rhythm of surmounting our struggles. Still, necessity may push us to a place in ourselves where we have never been, to an avenue of self-knowledge we would rather not traverse. We may have to summon our cumulative hardiness to venture in.

A woman in her early fifties recounted having been thrust into an awareness of herself she had not expected and at first could not encompass:

> I had this idea of who I was — nurturing, easygoing, flexible — the opposite of how my own mother had been. I really cherished this image. I considered myself the world's most supportive mother. In my late forties, I had a quarrel with my oldest daughter that rattled me to the core. She was saying how tired she was of trying to live up to all my expectations. I insisted it wasn't true, that I wasn't putting this on her. Then she hit me with a whole list of the ways she knew she fell short in my eyes. I was stunned. Somewhere inside, I saw that there might be some truth to what she was saying, but I wasn't ready to admit to it.

Her daughter's lament was a fundamental blow to her view of herself. Her first impulse was to fend it off, to show her daughter how wrong she was and how her complaint held little merit. The pain was so intense that she wanted to say awful things and withdraw. Instead, she held her tongue and asked for a cooling-off period.

At first, she just waited for her daughter to come to her senses. Then, she learned that everyone in her family felt they could never quite measure up. She began considering how she had managed to convey such exacting standards to her children. "For a while, I couldn't figure it out, how this could have happened. It was outside my awareness, completely against my intention." Reviewing an array of memories, she saw how her displeasure had unwittingly leaked out — through gestures that communicated disappointment, a tone of voice that expressed irritation, barbs disguised as jests. "It made me cry when I realized that what my daughter had said was true. Then I cried when I saw her finally relaxing in my company, after I eased up. She was able to just be herself."

This woman also saw how she had oppressed herself with excessively high expectations: "What I had been putting onto my kids was half of what I had been laying on myself over the years." She had carried a perpetual sense of not having made enough of herself, somehow not attaining all she had been meant to achieve. With the impact of these realizations, she was able to sit back and take stock of her own accomplishments for the first time. "I have the feeling of starting over, of taking things easier. It's a whole new life for me."

Making room within our self-conception for what comes to the surface on such occasions is a choice. We can gather up our hurts and doubts, daring to confront these uneasy layers of ourselves, or we can back away from further scrutiny. A willingness to be unsettled is essential to gaining new ground, and in later life we may have the verve to go through with it and allow ourselves to be shaken up.

Now in his mid-seventies, George Vaillant has spent most of his life exploring how people adapt to life's difficulties. He has overseen a longitudinal study of a group of Harvard men for several decades, interviewing them periodically and reviewing their responses to questionnaires. He has been particularly interested in the links between enduring early hardship and later-life success. How does travail turn into strength?

Vaillant's own father committed suicide when Vaillant was ten years old. He admits that carrying this burden kept him from becoming competent emotionally until his third marriage. As he was watching the men in the study endure, transcend, or sink under the weight of their difficulties, he was trying to comprehend the ways he was failing his children and hurting his intimate partners.

The men in the study who did the best in life were those who had experienced loving-kindness early on from someone — uncles, aunts, teachers, friends, neighbors — even if their parents had somehow failed to provide it. A basis for resilience seems to arise from having at least a single experience of positive, respectful regard. Even those with troubled beginnings did well if they had somehow acquired a vision of what goodness can be and how it can be manifested in relationships. This becomes a core strength, the grounding for later becoming a faithful partner, decent parent, and loyal friend.

Over the years, Vaillant gradually mastered his personal problems. He became more and more loving, and has been able to attain something like contentment. He told an interviewer he had learned "that the only thing that really matters in life are your relationships to other people."[3]

A 60-year-old man told me how he had emerged from a tumultuous youth: "I carry my mentors with me everywhere I go." Raised by an alcoholic single mother, he had been forced to live in a car with her each time they were evicted. He hung on to school for stability, often getting close to teachers by volunteering for special projects and staying after school as frequently as he could. At sixteen, he ran away and was eventually taken in by an uncle who lived in another state. His uncle was a gruff loner who nevertheless gave him devotion and constancy:

> He was a tough-love kind of guy — lots of toughness and some scraps of love here and there. Money would run right through my hands and he told me I wouldn't amount to anything that way. Being broke all the time — there's no self-respect in it. He showed me how to put money away so you couldn't spend it on a whim, even if that meant driving to a credit union in the next county. He died a long time ago, but I still keep my credit card inside a block of ice in my freezer. I know I can defrost it in an emergency. I have never bounced a check or been evicted, and you can bet I have money in the bank. My teachers are

still with me, too, because they gave me my first hope that I could have a good life.

As we get older, we acquire a host of tactics for enduring and adapting. Those who receive little bolstering early in life tend to gather in the many lessons of survival, using every kindness, learning all they can in order to prevail.

One morning, an older couple came into a café where I was writing. She led him to a table near mine and brought over the morning special — a plate of eggs with a piece of pastry. She gave him the eggs and put the pastry on a napkin for herself. Not a word was exchanged as they sat there looking out the window at the courtyard, savoring their food and each other. I could not resist them for long.

Shortly into our conversation I saw in his eyes that he was on the far end of dementia, knowing only that this was his wife and that he adored her. Married for fifty-three years, he was ninety-three and she was eighty-six. He was silent as she handled the nosy woman's questions. I asked if life had gotten better for them as they had gotten older. She stared at me. I tried to nudge her. Did she know more about life now?

"Now I think I know less." I started to take my leave of them after a few more futile promptings, but she held me back. "You know, I lived through the Depression. So I know things that have helped me, especially in the last few years. I got us moved to this neighborhood, like a village. We walk to everything. All that we need is right here. We can live."

This woman was grateful that she could still take care of her husband and that they were still together. She had chosen a section of the city where services were within reach and there was plenty to do every day. On a fixed income, she was taking advantage of her long habit of thrift. A few weeks later, I returned to the neighborhood and saw them walking hand in hand down the street. She was glancing in shop windows, and he was holding on to her for dear life.

14
COHERENCE

Life and the memory of it so compressed they've turned into each other. Which is which?

ELIZABETH BISHOP

A life story is like an Impressionist painting, a riot of tiny brushstrokes when viewed up close. There is a great deal we are unable to discern about our lives while we are still caught up in the small exertions of living. Getting older allows us to step back far enough to recognize the overall shape of things, the full picture that can only be seen from the distance of an elapsed lifetime. Our most wrenching experiences gain particular clarity in retrospect. Relationships with people forsaken or misperceived, hurts or disappointments we thought we had settled long ago, call out to be explored anew. An overarching view thus becomes one of the gifts of aging.

182

Oscar Sheppler, a philosophy professor nearing retirement, engaged in a lively dialogue about the stereotypes of aging with a former student entering middle age. Professor Sheppler insisted that past, present, and future orientations are not separate in us, but overlapping:

> To think in absolute terms, young, old, is misleading. We are, at every moment, younger and older. . . . Only we, as we become more aware of physical change, mistakenly identify aging with deterioration, with progress toward death, not fulfillment of life. That's where we've gone wrong in our thinking. . . . [Perhaps] we harbor old age within us. And if we have the proper understanding, this inner sage is no grim reaper but a principle of life, of continuous renewal.[1]

Sometime before records and turntables started vanishing, I came across an old record labeled "All Long Island Youth Orchestra Annual Spring Concert, 1967." Due to a dire shortage of violas, I had been drafted into that premier orchestra while the best violinist in our school had to audition to get in. It was exciting to wear a black velvet skirt and fancy white blouse, and to sit on the stage of a real concert hall. As for playing, I was relieved that the other three violists were somewhat competent. This meant I could put as little pressure on the bow as possible, minimizing the risk of ruining the sound made by my more skillful compatriots.

I slipped the record onto the turntable and lowered the stylus, eager to hear our proud little orchestra. It was awful — out of tune, out of sync, close to intolerable. I tried the other side, and it was just as bad or worse. My memory of magnificence was replaced by discordance. I regretted having played the record, since I knew I could never reinstall the remembrance in my mind that had been so much better than the reality. My crowning moment had been reduced to something pitiful.

That night, however, my parents had made me feel like a princess. They handed me a bouquet of flowers when I found them in the lobby afterward, telling me how wonderful the concert had been and how proud they were of seeing me up on that stage. They took me out for ice cream at a fancy diner afterward — only me, since my siblings had been left home with a baby-sitter. This was the only time I had ever been taken out for a treat by myself. I was in my 14-year-old splendor sitting at the booth with a triple-scoop hot fudge sundae topped by a mountain of whipped cream.

As I was putting away the record, it occurred to me that my parents had done a fine job creating the majesty of that night. Underneath the groaning sound of the orchestra, carried almost thirty years forward in time, my parents' dedication had come through loud and clear. The music may have been off-key, but their performance displayed perfect parental pitch. My mother had taken me to Macy's for the expensive skirt and blouse, despite their scarcity of funds raising four kids on a junior high school teacher's salary. My father had driven me diligently to several Saturday rehearsals a long way from home. They had taken on the cost of the babysitter, the flowers, and plunking down even more cash for the recording of the great event.

As we live our lives, thousands of small victories are lost to memory. I can now see the neat stack of underwear and socks that appeared reliably on my dresser, the labor of my mother's hands clean and fresh from the dryer. There was always a loaf of bread on the kitchen counter and something to put between the slices for the sandwich that filled my metal lunch box. For Chanukah, each child received a neatly wrapped gift every night for eight nights in a row. I never did the math back then to herald the marvel of thirty-two gifts procured and wrapped so beautifully. Finally, I am old enough to respect that my mother hauled herself out of bed every morning and pushed herself through an unhappy marriage until her children were grown.

There was so much strife in our household that I have been prone to overlook the strengths. This aging piece of circular plastic held evidence of what was sturdy in my parents, how they had been able to pull themselves together and function in all the most important ways. The grooves held reverberations of what it meant to have had two parents who put their children at the center of their lives, proof of the abiding support and love that was the backdrop of my days. This was the real story in the spring of 1967.

Asking our parents to expand on stories from their early life history sometimes goes against the grain — theirs and ours. We may have endured certain stories many times before, fixed versions repeated verbatim at family gatherings that tend to obscure more than they reveal. In his youth, my husband had asked his parents many times why they had lingered for five years in the Displaced Persons camp instead of coming to this country right after the war. Their replies were always insufficient or evasive.

Turning forty, he tried again. His parents were nearing their seventies, and he sensed that they might be ready to assemble their privations and triumphs into a real story. Barry, too, had changed. Where once he would have barged headlong into his parents' obfuscations, his tone had become gentle. Where he would have despaired about ever knowing their full story, he had accepted what could not be spoken.

Out came the shame and hurt of their having been among the last to leave their DP camp after the war. Initially, a wealthy relative in New York City had refused to sponsor them. It took a few years to locate the impoverished cousin in Florida who finally agreed to assist them. Over the years since that time, his parents had heard the accounts of many others who had trouble finding relatives or friends willing to sign the required promises of financial support. Overall, there was a shortage of people willing to house newcomers who spoke no English and arrived with only the clothes on their backs. Rather than a personal embarrassment, they had come to see their early situation as comparable to thousands of others who had been derided as greenhorns and scorned because of their poverty.

At the same time that Barry's need to know had changed, his parents' need to tell had evolved. Both Barry and his parents had deepened into who they had become, with the passage of time feeding their realizations and extending the reach of their compassion for one another. His tender inquiry suggested the possibility of long-awaited comprehension, and his parents responded.

When a parent detects sympathy coming from a grown child, a hope for new closeness quickly arises. An adult son or daughter asking questions without a hint of accusation is a powerful inducement for a parent to open up. In itself, a son or daughter's receptivity may draw out the parent's memories, and further details may come to the surface. Formerly inarticulate emotions may suddenly enter their recollections. Under these circumstances, a tale may attain new clarity, without the blurring of defensiveness or self-justification. Painful feelings a parent had borne alone may be finally witnessed and assuaged. This may be the first time an important family story is told with any depth.

A 57-year-old man knew little about his father's childhood, except that his grandfather had gone off to World War I when his father was an infant:

Raising us, my dad showed no emotion, only toughness. All he ever did was give orders and pick at us — to make our rooms neater, to get our homework done faster, to do our chores better. He growled instead of talking. There was never any praise, not a drop of affection. I considered him an unfeeling autocrat and got away from him as soon as I could. About a year ago, I happened to watch a program about trench warfare. They showed photos of the soldiers' faces, shell-shocked and broken, and it hit me that my dad was raised by a father like that. I had heard stories, but never connected the dots before. His father must have been blank, like a robot. My dad had learned about being a father from a shattered man. The anger I'd been carrying all these years drained out of me. I just felt bad for him. I felt bad for myself.

A few months after having this realization, he visited his father for Thanksgiving. The 83-year-old readily assented to taking a long walk after dinner, just the two of them. "I told him about the program I'd watched and how I had imagined his father being like a zombie with his little boy when he came home from the war. My dad started sobbing. I couldn't believe it, out there on a quiet county road. I put my arm around him and he cried his heart out. Then he told me a bunch of stories about his growing up that I'd never heard before, each one of them really heartbreaking."

From that point on, their relationship had a strong undercurrent of warmth. His father was still awkward with expressing affection or giving praise, but the son could detect what was flowing beneath the surface. "It might sound really strange, but now I can feel what's going on during his silences. When he does say something, I catch different tones in his voice. It's like the emotion was there all along, but now I can read him." The inheritance of World War I was finally coming to a close.

One afternoon, I was helping a woman nearing one hundred sort through a huge pile of medical bills. She startled me in the midst of our task by asking if there might have been a connection between her older brother "bothering" her sexually when she was a little girl and her never having enjoyed intimacy with her husband. "They have a name for it now," she told me. "You see, it happened to Oprah. They call it sexual abuse."

There we were, at her kitchen table in a tiny studio apartment. It was almost ninety years since her brother had first molested her, and the first time that she had spoken of it. I responded fervently: "You were a sweet, innocent girl. Nothing was ever wrong with you. Those memories naturally interfered later on. Now help is available they didn't have back then. It would be totally different these days." There was a long silence between us. I heard the ticking of the clock in the hallway. "I have a lot to think about," she said with a deep sigh.

I was supposed to be matching itemized bills and statements of benefits, and instead I was helping her rearrange the way she viewed her life. It seemed the vast burden of her secret was shifting before my eyes. The concept of having been wronged is a far cry from believing in the idea of having been born tainted.

In isolation, shame intensifies. We make more of it through our fear of other people's scorn and years of lonely rumination. A small child's readiness to take the blame gets sealed off from corrective feedback. This woman had carried the idea of herself as sexually defective for so long that it eventually became an entrenched part of her self-image, until she heard Oprah name her experience as one shared by many others.

When I was a hospice social worker, I was regularly privy to such confessions. I learned that heartbreak is not over until it is told. Last-minute attempts to encompass old agonies with understanding are part of the terrain of dying. I learned to hang around at the kitchen table or bedside, assisting with paperwork, phone calls to insurance companies, and the like, on the chance that the readiness to speak might arise. I would convey my receptivity in subtle ways, dropping questions that could be brushed off or taken as invitations to enter deep subjects.

The stories that we cordon off become like blank spaces on a map, without roads or any ready means of access. Those who set aside their worst experiences, vowing never to speak of them, are shaped by this avoidance. Unexpressed pain does not evolve. Positive emotions may remain constricted as well; detachment may mar times that would have been celebratory. Guarding against bad memories can become a self-created sense of removal.

A woman facing a terminal illness in her mid-seventies told me about once driving drunk with her three young sons in her car. She had carried this story for almost fifty years, holding on to it through hundreds of AA meetings during her decades of sobriety, never able to give voice to the agony of this failure. She told me how she had taken to drink after her young husband was killed in a car accident. "It was more than you could bear," I responded. She looked at me, astonished, and then wept as hard as I have ever seen anyone weep. There were moments when she could not catch her breath through her heaving sobs. Her frail body shook so violently I worried that she might die then and there.

When she calmed down, she said she had always considered herself a terrible person. Self-hatred had affected every day of her life since she succumbed to alcohol, and continued as an undercurrent during her many years of sobriety. When I saw her a few weeks later, her face had shed deep lines of worry and pain. She said she had been rethinking her past, and that this was the first time she had felt anything like tranquility since her husband's death.

We yearn to be known before we go. Many

wait until death is near before going back to the furthest reaches of their soul and revealing what happened years ago. A tale of grief too long contained may burst forth at the last minute for the sake of being seen and dying whole. Whenever I listen to a story like this, I feel as though a corridor has opened back through the decades to the youth of the person in front of me.

My mother had long been unable to talk about having been raped at knifepoint at the age of twenty-three. Near the end of her life, I read a passage to her from a book written by a young woman who had been forced into a back room in a suburban laundromat on a sunny Saturday morning and raped with a knife held to her throat. The author told of the unspeakable isolation that had resulted from her rape, a sense of having been cut off from the human community. My mother grabbed the book and held it to her chest. It was one of the closest moments we ever had as mother and daughter.

We reach later life noticing the ways we have made do with surfaces, when there may have been so much more there for the taking. We see the degree to which we have allowed ourselves to be loved without being known, and how much more we could have loved those we thought we knew. The readiness to take another look arises in the delicate interplay between the desire to be known and the hope of being understood.

15
STORIES

The great thing about getting older is that you don't lose all the other ages you've been.

MADELEINE L'ENGLE

Telling stories about a past that has finally been grasped is one of the triumphs of duration. Until we have lived long enough, we do not realize how extensively our recollections get shifted and rearranged over time. The flux arises not so much from revising our memories as revisiting them. We go back and look around with new eyes, each time seeing more of what is there. We infuse what we have learned since into what we did not know at the time, and things begin to make a further kind of sense. With fresh sympathy for those who populate our recollections, the past transforms because *we* are changing. We know so much more.

At the age of sixty-nine, a man stumbled

upon a cache of stories he did not know he had inside him. His 10-year-old granddaughter had spurred him on with loving but persistent questions:

My granddaughter wants to know everything. Not just where I grew up, but what kind of dog I had and what chores did I have to do and what I was thinking after my father died. She's quite the detective. I have so many stories, so many memories I didn't know were there. It's like she's bringing my life back to me. I was almost her age when my father died. She's bringing him back to me.

Each tale took him back to the time when he had been a boy who had a father, the very memories he had forbidden himself ever since his father's death. Wanting to be strong for his mother's sake, he had barricaded himself from his feelings. "No wonder I was always accused of being too serious." Gazing at his granddaughter's innocence, he saw the enormity of the loss that must have filled his eyes at that age. Entwined in a jumble of reclaimed emotions was a life story that could finally be told.

■ ■ ■ ■

Whenever a cat threatens to jump onto my lap, I am terrified. People find this amusing. Many have tried to cure me of my fear, to no avail. The roots of it go back to early childhood, to a time without words, when a cat must have dug his claws into me and not let go. This is what I fear. At dinner parties in houses presided over by a cat, I always keep a bulky purse on my lap as a blockade and sit tight up against the table.

The whole time, I know that the cat is aware of what I am doing and why I am doing it. My fear is so alluring that the cat will invariably sit at my feet under the table throughout the meal, awaiting an opportunity. Occasionally, during the post-dinner mingling in the living room, I drop my guard. I flop down on a sofa and put down my purse. Pounce. The cat lands on my lap. My terror becomes everyone's hilarity.

Some traumatic events leave marks on us that are beyond words and reason. There can be a lessening of intensity over the years, but such imprinting is essentially timeless. Our strongest feelings are etched onto the amygdala, a part of the brain that becomes disconnected under duress, losing contact with the regions that would have supplied a chronological context or broader understanding. Later, emotions may seem to come out of the blue, containing whispers of memories or fragmented images, but not enough to make a complete tale. We are left with reflex, the way we spring back from a hot pan we touch accidentally. It is the felt reality of existence without explanation.

Turning an onerous event into a story changes it into something we can bear. When we are able to tell a story that has been long silent, additional blood flows to the cerebral structures where meaning is made. The hippocampus becomes activated, providing a context in time and place as we put experiences into words. The accompanying emotions no longer seem to feel like harbingers of secret sorrow. The pain may become vivid again, but this time there is comfort and perhaps lucidity.

A woman in her mid-eighties told me she endured years of recurrent depression and anxiety before she was able to tell the story of her childhood in a comprehensive way. The basic frame of it was clear — her mother had blamed her for her sister's death when she was six and her sister was eight — but there were many layers appended to this structure that had to be stripped away. The process took her almost seventy years.

Her sister stumbled on some stairs after retrieving an item they needed for a fort they were building outside. Two weeks later she died from spinal meningitis, not from the slight injury incurred during the fall. Their distraught mother told her, "If you hadn't made her go back into the house, she wouldn't have fallen and gotten sick." Their father blamed their mother for her inadequate supervision, and the household fell into a period of darkness. Six years later, the birth of a son called the parents back to life. At twelve, she watched her little brother receive all the cherishing that she had come to live without.

When she became a mother herself, she understood how her mother found the senselessness of the loss unbearable — even to the point of clinging to an explanation that sacrificed her other child. Her mother could not look at her without being reminded of the terrible sorrow. Still, self-blame and the unanswered need for nurturance remained pervasive themes in all her relationships. It was not until she became an elder that she was able to tell the story of her sister's death without shouldering the terrible burden that had been placed on her. She tells the story now in a few sentences, and there is only a trace of the agony and self-blame she carried for so long.

For most of our lives, we are preoccupied by the future. Looking forward seems far more interesting than looking back. All that can yet happen intrigues us, while the past seems fixed and airless. Gradually, our future gets so much smaller than our enlarging past that we are forced to shift our gaze. Just as a society derives its heft more from its history than its hopes, we come to suspect that what we have already experienced is our treasure trove.

When she was in her early seventies, Carter Catlett Williams decided it was time to retrieve an old box of letters from her attic. Most of the letters were written by her father to his parents from his days at boarding school, West Point, and an Army Air Service base in Hawaii. His plane crashed in 1925, when his only daughter was twenty-two months old. She had no idea that reading her father's letters would provoke a transformation unlike any other in her life.

Transcribing and organizing the letters took several years. Hearing his written voice, she got to know the father she was unable to remember. She was moved to tears as she read his minute descriptions of his little daughter's gestures and her first utterances, realizing that her father's affection had shaped her emotional core.

At times, she wished she had read the letters years earlier, but came to realize "this stage of life may be the best time for something that goes so deeply into the heart and bears such fruit."

No amount of hearing about my father could bring him to me, into my life, as reading his own words has. His thoughts, hopes, miseries, passions, uncertainties and delights poured out on paper three-quarters of a century ago have brought encounters between the two of us. . . . My father's letters have given me new life to be reckoned with and reconsideration of the old.[1]

During this process of discovery, she found routes for releasing the pent-up sorrow she did not know that she carried. She was able to reveal parts of herself to her husband and adult children that had been rendered unreachable by her prolonged disconnection from this grief. The revelations just kept on coming, along with fresh emotion, as her account of her father attained its fullest elaboration. She found uncanny similarities in their views of social justice, faith, family allegiances, and the power of the written word. In the subterranean reaches where love resides, she saw that she had been accompanied by her father all along.

Later life is when we need stories the most. It is not only about having the time and mustering the courage to return to a past that has been sequestered, but also sensing the parts of ourselves that still ache to be comforted. The act of articulation gives suffering a route to repose.

Evelyn, my mother-in-law, kept the worst stories of her flight from the Nazis to herself, even in the last months of her life. At the memorial, a hospice worker who had come three times a week to help her bathe said, "I am here tonight to tell all of you that the tears of the Holocaust were cried into the bathwater. With each bath, she told me such terrible stories. I wanted you to know." The sensation of the warm washcloth as June soaped her back, her gentle fingers massaging her scalp and washing her hair, brought out the stories that she could never tell us.

Near the end, when the right kind of listener appears, there is no time to waste. Ideally, we risk opening our hearts to loved ones, but what matters is that our stories get heard in whatever way possible. Often, it is easier to tell a stranger, and this suffices. A stranger's reaction may feel safer for being less evocative. There is no fear of further questions, no entanglement with explanations — just a long-awaited surfacing of that which has been too long underground.

Once we have a willing listener, such recounting may become an actual re-experiencing of the past. The original emotions may arise with surprising force. When we are not alone with what is being recalled so vividly, we alter the tenor of our memories. It is never too late to tell a story and come to peace.

The right kind of listener makes a difference. When someone takes the time to hear us out, something singular happens. By being interested and showing it, the listener becomes part of the tale. Commiserating, laughing, asking questions — these responses draw out further feelings embedded in the nuances. Stretching out a good tale, feeling for the details and recounting them to the right extent, makes the difference between an interlude of discovery and bland recital.

Ideally, reactions are handed back and forth as the one remembering is spurred on by the one receiving the memories. Reflection then fulfills the double meaning of having our thoughts mirrored in dialogue and getting to reach more deeply into the silences. The gaps in our tales then become doorways, pauses during which we receive intimations from what has been half forgotten.

For painful subjects, especially, we need to spin out our stories without the threat of interruption. To work through a snag in a relationship, it is best to let go of urgency. Tangled feelings do not sort out on demand. They shrink from our grasp, the more ardently we try to extract them. Couples who give each other this kind of time replenish their consonance. With an exchange of open-ended listening, something tight in both people loosens. On a long walk with all devices turned off, time together is assured by the distance traversed. Both people can risk entering into complicated terrain, knowing there will be time to find their way through.

Recently, I took a road trip with an old friend in which our destination required driving almost six hours each way. We took turns telling stories and exchanging observations from having witnessed twenty-five years of each other's life. We went from one subject to another, following tributaries here and there, sometimes returning to where a particular stream originated and sometimes not. My friend and I found that our dialogue fostered realizations in many directions at once, in such a torrent that it seemed our journey only took a couple of hours.

Digressions allow us to bump into unexpected perspectives. If we let our thoughts and feelings meander, we end up far afield from where we began. The listener responds with a countering idea or a question, and we are deflected in yet another direction. Then a previously vague idea becomes a thought, fully formed. The banter quickens. We mix in the new perceptions that keep arising. Soon it seems as though we have arrived at where we needed to go and that we may have been heading there all along.

Pondering out loud is often uncanny. Thanks to the inducement of someone's warmth and interest, we may re-enter a memory as never before. We may be able to recall details of what happened and feel the import of the event anew. Revelations keep mounting. Aspects of the experience that had been long forgotten may be called to consciousness; connections between events that had seemed unrelated may become clear. The teller of such a story and the listener join as complexities fall into place and meaning is made. We may hear ourselves voicing an insight that arises as we speak, springing up through the sheer act of articulation. Out may burst another kind of story altogether.

My father-in-law had chest pain in his early eighties that he refused to have investigated. One night, he held his teen-aged grandchildren to the dinner table long after dessert, telling a long, intricate tale about his survival after fleeing the Nazi invasion of Poland. He went into detail about each act of kindness he experienced during a winter when he wandered in search of food and shelter. He described the rags he tied to his feet for some protection from the snowy ground, and how he celebrated when he found a piece of rubber to serve as a bottom layer amidst the rags. Until it wore out, he gained a few weeks' respite for his aching feet.

One day he traded the shirt he was wearing for a loaf of bread. For one afternoon, he would not be hungry. He walked barechested down the road knowing that by nightfall he could easily freeze to death. He tried to move as quickly as possible to generate warmth. His only hope was to find a barn where he could burrow that night in the hay. A merchant driving a horse-drawn wagon happened by and gave him both a ride and a shirt. They rode together for several days. Half a lifetime later, Izzie happened to run into this man in the Miami area. He had also settled there after the war, but had not had good fortune and was in poor health. Izzie gave him a room in the apartment hotel he was managing and looked after him until he died.

A massive heart attack took Izzie a few weeks after he told this story, but he had managed to recount it all to his grandchildren. I thought back to the way he had told it — as though he was conveying the most important lesson of his long life. Among all of his tribulations, a single act of kindness had stood out. At one point, the children had squirmed a bit during one of the many layers of the tale, and he leaned forward and growled: *Remember this.* He wanted them to keep this lesson in kindness with them all of their lives, as it had stayed with him. He hoped they would grow up to become the kind of people who would give a freezing man a shirt.

16
CHANGING COURSE

Life would be infinitely happier if we could only be born at the age of eighty and gradually approach eighteen.

MARK TWAIN

The urgency inherent in getting older often produces corrective energy. We may find it impossible to carry out one more obfuscation or indulge in yet another delaying tactic. This does not mean renouncing regret as much as accepting what it has to teach us. What we can grasp at fifty highlights all we misperceived at twenty and may foster an interest in changing course.

It is exciting to snap out of avoidance. Compromises tolerated for too long can be overthrown; dilemmas evaded for decades can be unraveled. We may find that facing our flaws, subjecting ourselves to inner scrutiny, is the long-awaited antidote to hurting from what we wish we could have done differently. We may realize the time has come to take a few faltering steps into the unknown, to allow something to happen beyond the safety of our previous certainty.

As a child, I remember how disputes in games on the playground would be resolved with a *do-over*. There was a certain glee in clearing the slate. The ball would be returned to where it had been, each of us would take up our original positions, and we would get another chance. *Ready, set, go.* We would put all we had into it.

Years ago, I met someone at a conference who handed me a useful definition of denial: *Replacing reality with something more pleasurable.* The things we do not want to face slip into the netherworld of unawareness, replaced by something easier to bear. Since the evasion is not deliberate, we do not have to feel guilty. We just get angry at anyone who tries to interfere with our improved version of reality. It is human nature to deal with difficult matters when we are ready, and not a minute sooner.

Underneath, the problems we have set aside await our attention. Newer versions of the same problems arise and get added to the accumulation. We may remain insulated, but a quiet pressure builds inside us. Eventually, something happens to thrust it all forward in a form that cannot be denied, such as a partner's fury, a daughter's hurt, or a surprising turn in a conversation with a stranger.

At a social gathering several years ago, I was seated next to someone in his early fifties who told me about his high-profile job. I asked whether he felt fulfilled. He looked at me, somewhat perplexed by the question, because his work was national in scope and widely esteemed. He told me it certainly was sweet to be at the height of his career, that he had attained virtually everything he had always wanted professionally. We went on to talk about the tricky balance between family life and work responsibilities. He became more and more wistful, the longer we talked about our lives. He admitted that he had missed out on many celebratory events in his children's lives and that he could use some time to renew his relationship with his wife.

Admitting dissatisfaction out loud often serves as the opening of a valve. Once it has been spoken, a truth that has been kept safely sequestered may flow out in many manifestations. Further containment becomes impossible. We may try to avoid focusing on what is coming up, but the thoughts are there waiting for unguarded moments, such as while taking a shower or going for a run. We find ourselves facing what we have long known but not wanted to see.

About a year later, I read in the newspaper that this man had accepted a demotion to a less prestigious but more on-the-ground aspect of his field, where he said his passion had always been. Our conversation may have had nothing to do with this change in his life, but I suspect his facade of contentment began to disintegrate that night. It is likely that from then on he was unable to go on pretending, at least not to himself.

When I was in my late twenties, I was invited to sit in on a meeting of high-powered leaders. They had some critical decisions to make. To my dismay, their discussion quickly devolved into a contest of wills. There was posturing and pontificating, with little listening or inquiry. Each person was seeking to convince the others, and no one was conceding the possibility that another's view might be more useful than their own.

As the allotted time was drawing to a close, everyone at the table was visibly frustrated by the lack of progress. Several were clearly incensed that their particular ideas had not been heeded by the group. The level of tension was high. In my estimation, something had gone terribly wrong. I was too inexperienced to know that this almost always happens when such a group convenes, that nothing unusual had taken place.

The only other observer present was a man in his early sixties. I watched him writing steadily throughout the meeting, not saying a word, but filling many pages of a yellow pad with his elegant script. Finally, he asked if he could offer some observations. Everyone fell silent. One by one, he summarized the ideas that had been offered by each person. Then he pointed out where there had been a measure of consonance here and there. Suddenly, excitement erupted as a useful compromise became evident to all. There was a burst of discussion, and the meeting concluded with a workable plan.

Afterward, I went for a walk with this magician. I had to know how he had pulled the rabbit out of his hat. He replied with a story. When he was fifty-six, the company he led was taken over by a conglomerate and he was promptly cast out. His standard of living plummeted along with his self-respect. Month after month, he would make it to the final round of job interviews, only to see younger people get hired in his stead. Each rejection sent him lower. It became clear that his years of experience worked against him, with employers favoring those they perceived as more malleable. "It took me a while, but I had to stop trying to re-create the life I had before."

He finally took a job on a house-painting crew, just to have some income coming in and to shake off his growing despondency. Each morning, the crew chief would gather everyone together and let them hash out the day's assignments. The workers had a real say in how things went, within the parameters set by the chief. "It was amazing. That guy managed to get sustained effort out of each one of us without being heavy-handed at all." This former leader then perceived his own management style clearly for the first time:

I was the boss and everyone had to know it. My suggestions were really orders, just sugarcoated. I would make a great show of soliciting other people's ideas and contributions, but the only counsel I actually heeded was my own. I hoped my staff respected me, but it didn't really matter. I wanted their compliance most of all. I used the lingo of teamwork and all that, and I saw myself as the enlightened one. It was an illusory world, with me at the center, perpetually stressed and exhausted.

One morning he was perched on a ladder, paintbrush in hand, and he came to the realization that changed his life: "The less you are interested in power, the more you have." He was so startled that he barely avoided a fall. He decided to start a consultancy helping midlevel managers revive staff morale, teaching them how to run meetings that get somewhere and ways to make sure everyone gets to contribute to decisions that matter to them. "I demonstrate listening, putting yourself aside so that you can hear what other people are saying — the mirror image of my previous approach."

He told me that each session that he conducts reveals more about his earlier failings. This is the humiliating aspect of growth — to look back and see our prior limitations as we surpass them. "My wife likes this new version of me quite a bit. I like this guy so much better than that fellow who was full of ego and hot air."

A woman in her late fifties often took off

from work in order to accompany her mother to chemotherapy sessions for breast cancer. She preferred this much more than the evenings when she prepared dinner for her parents, because she disliked being around her aloof father. He would often hover by her in the kitchen, standing there stiffly, saying nothing and making her nervous. She would experiment with recipes to entice her mother to eat, all the while wishing he would leave the kitchen.

What she did not know was that her father was utterly moved by her devotion. He would stay there beside her at the kitchen counter with tears in his eyes that she could not see and gratitude toward her that he could not voice. Emotional walls he had hidden behind since boyhood were coming down. Raised by a sharp-tongued, cruel father, he had learned to keep his most vulnerable feelings out of sight. Watching her prepare intricate sauces and creative salads, he wanted to tell her how much he loved and respected her.

The capacity to be openhearted is there for all of us in childhood, but is easily damaged by harsh treatment. As adults, some people can only tolerate friendships that stay on the surface, partners who ask for little outside of bed, or relationships with adult children that keep a safe distance. Later in life, there is often a time of emotional reopening, especially when the need for kindness arises and is met with sensitivity and grace. This father did not have the vocabulary for feelings, yet he was bursting with things to say to his thoughtful, hardworking daughter.

Several months later, she found herself thrown together with him again as they maintained a twenty-four-hour vigil in her mother's hospital room. They took turns dozing in the recliner beside her bed. For hours on end, they listened to her ragged breathing. Every so often, one would gently put a few ice chips in her mouth and the other would moisten her lips with a mint-flavored swab. Shortly before dying, her mother called out his name through the haze of morphine. He broke down sobbing across her chest, and the daughter draped her arms around her parents and wept into the back of her father's shirt.

This father and daughter ended up with a closeness that far exceeded anything she had ever thought possible. He did not become demonstrative, verbally or physically, but his eyes and his manner became tender. "He was different all the way around," she said. "He became the dad I always wanted. I just

wish Mom could have seen him like that."
They stayed close until he died a few years
later.

A life-changing epiphany cannot be summoned, as much as we might yearn for one.
Often, what leads us into transformation
accrues gradually, resulting from the hard
work of decades as insight builds in small
increments. We go about our daily lives and
there is a melding of forces inside us, a
growing readiness that may suddenly culminate in a startling shift of awareness. Throwing off what had fettered us for so many
years is the privilege of having evolved and
thus can have a galvanizing power. We only
wonder what took us so long.

About to turn fifty, a friend of mine had
been garnering national recognition for his
writing and public speaking. He had attained a measure of fame, but all along had
been contending with an undercurrent of
deep unease. Recently, I saw him again after
a two-year gap. As soon as I glimpsed his
face, I knew that something remarkable had
occurred. He was eager to explain:

One day I was driving in my truck, just running errands, and it hit me that I was going to die. This came to me completely out

of the blue, for no particular reason — but I was slammed in the gut. I saw that I had twenty, maybe thirty years left, if all went well. Before this moment, death had been purely theoretical. Suddenly it became personal. Then a kind of serenity came over me, a feeling of relief. Had I been seeking immortality? Whatever it was that had been ruling me, it was over. I didn't have to keep pushing so hard.

He began declining commitments that took him too far from home. He started to orient himself toward his family, rather than the career that had been claiming most of his attention for more than three decades. Almost immediately, his marriage prospered from this relocation of his focus. He had ceased his constant striving for a wider reach, a bigger audience that might prevent his eventual obscurity. He felt that there was no attainment out on the road that could compare with what was available to him at home.

Having quietly acquired multiple levels of awareness, we may be surprised by the depth of comprehension that comes to us as we get older. Thirty years later, a mother raped at knifepoint in her youth may be able to show vulnerability instead of anger. A daughter may finally see how helplessness, rather than any intent to harm, animated her mother's failings. Openhearted sympathy for each other may lead to solace, at long last.

Alchemists employed the concept *opus contra naturam,* an idea which Jung refashioned as a struggle against our own nature. The heat of difficult experiences often transforms our engagement in living, such that something better results. Loss supplies the energy for transformation, and an attitude of determination carries us through doubt. By welcoming risk and learning all we can from our blunders, we ensure that any detours will lead back around to a life we can respect. Then later life may far surpass what came before.

■ ■ ■ ■

PART THREE: PEACE

■ ■ ■ ■

17
Courage

Life is either a daring adventure, or
nothing.

HELEN KELLER

A 96-year-old woman explained that she
did not become courageous until her late
fifties, but then there was no stopping her:

I was the proverbial good little girl, totally
bound up in what was expected of me.
The last thing I wanted was to call attention to myself by stepping out of line, rocking the boat. I had to reach the point where
I just didn't care. Once I broke free, I suppose I got a bit wild for a while. I loved
breaking the rules. I could spit on the
sidewalk if I felt like it. I had to defy every
rule I ran into. My kids were embarrassed
by me. Gradually, I got bored of rebelling.
My sixties were fabulous. I found my own
interests and I'm still taking it from there.

We might admire those who climb mountains in their seventies, but the most important kinds of courage are internal. Fears that have stood in our way for years often succumb to later-life bravery. We take on these fears, not only because they have shrunk in our estimation, but also because other constraints on our spirit have fallen away. Changes on so many fronts at once have compelled us to be flexible with our expectations and to adapt to the unforeseen. So much has been altered and rearranged that we may cease holding parts of ourselves in reserve. We are torn loose.

Imogen Cunningham, the photographer, did not begin to attain fame until her seventies and eighties. After being repeatedly turned down for a Guggenheim grant at this stage in her life, she flew to the Guggenheim offices and harassed them into giving her a grant at the age of eighty-seven.[1]

The routes to courage in later life are varied, idiosyncratic, and available to all who would dare proceed. At a certain point, we recognize that the uses for prudence have expired. With each successive loss, our grip on our remaining attachments slackens. We are ready to throw caution to the wind.

In my youth, I had an extreme terror of

public speaking. Just the thought of raising my hand in a college class made my heart thump rapidly in my chest. Having to introduce myself as we went around the circle in graduate school seminars had me trembling and hyperventilating. Standing up to deliver a presentation in front of the whole class was nothing less than torture, intensified by a dry mouth and a stiff, immobilized neck. For a while, I considered dropping out of graduate school to avoid the humiliation.

Inexplicably, the desire to teach took precedence over the fear. A mentor told me the cure was cognitive and behavioral, detaching the response from the stimulus. I had to do it over and over again, he said, until the sight of faces looking at me no longer triggered the terror. For practice, I pushed through my nervousness in front of groups of four or five students who wanted to learn the art of résumé and cover-letter preparation. Then I taught groups of ten or twelve nursing assistants about how to deal with difficult people. Eventually, I was able to handle leading workshops in front of thirty or forty social work and nursing colleagues. Ten years later, I still trembled and took gasping breaths at the beginning of every program, but my agony became less intense and did not last as long.

One day, I arrived at a professional conference the afternoon before I was to lead a few workshops. The organizer met me at the hotel's front desk to ask if I would deliver the opening keynote address the next morning, as the scheduled presenter had canceled due to illness. The idea of standing up in front of five hundred people sent me back to the starting line of my struggle, but I agreed to do it. I was weary of the fear, tired of having to keep fighting through it. I wanted to take it to the mat.

I did not sleep at all that night. The speech played and replayed in my head, and the anxiety was electric. Shortly after dawn, I had security unlock the lecture hall where I was to meet my fear three hours later. I stood at the podium, facing the rows and rows of empty seats. *Everyone who enters this room will one day be dead.* This was the thought that calmed me down. There was nothing to be afraid of, really, since eventually no one would be alive who heard me give the speech that day. Later, as person after person filed in, taking their seats, I put them in coffins and buried them. It was an exhausting mental project, but I remained in a surprisingly tranquil state of mind. Then I stood up and gave one of the finest talks I have ever given, receiving a standing ovation and enthusiastic testimonies from the people who formed a long line afterward to thank me.

Later that year, I began accepting invitations to deliver keynote speeches at national conferences. By the time I turned fifty, ten years later, I no longer had to bury each person individually before speaking. I still find it necessary to visualize my own death in order to speak comfortably. In front of big audiences, I must enter the calm of my ultimate insignificance.

Courage in later life has a lot to do with letting go. James Hillman, the Jungian psychologist, claimed at age seventy-three: "You're more flexible, you can go with life, you can receive life . . . once you've let down your own fixed positions — which tend to be defenses, refusals to let anything else in."[2] Holding tightly to ingrained attitudes leaves us stuck and tired, while yielding may propel us to a breakthrough.

A 69-year-old man fell, hit his head, and almost died. At the hospital, when it was still not certain if he would survive, his ex-wife came to see him. To their mutual astonishment, they found that many of their barricades had fallen away:

I was shocked to wake up and see her there, standing beside my bed. At first, I thought I was delirious. We hadn't seen each other in such a long time. She was so loving. I think it shook her up to see me like that, with the bandages and the tubes and all that. We really talked, like we hadn't in years and years. It wasn't like old times, exactly, but it was something really special. I'm telling you, it was worth almost dying.

Once we are jolted out of our usual manner of being and responding, we may throw up our hands emotionally and let go. What is there to lose in this realm anymore? Especially when illness exposes us to need, we may enter an unnerving time of appraisal. Grudges, resentments, old recriminations — the effort necessary for their maintenance seems better applied to something life-giving. In some instances, we have become so detached from a long-standing bitterness that we cannot even recall how it got started. We look around at our relationships and wonder who will come through for us, whom we can call upon for help. We may be forced to venture beyond the well-worn path we have been on in order to place ourselves within reach of sustenance, warmth, and hope. It may be time to let ourselves get carried away.

Told she could no longer drive, a woman in her late sixties at first refused offers of rides. She sat at home and raged at the world: "I can't stand the idea of waiting to be picked up, of being on someone else's schedule, going where they want to go. I can't tolerate doing things at other people's behest." I knew her fury to be grief, and hoped she would speedily move through it to the other side.

At first, the compromises that come with accepting help may be out of the question. We naturally rail against anything that signals decrepitude, and it seems absurd to expose our vulnerability, disrupt our privacy, or lose control over the timing of our preferences. It is tempting to quit long-beloved involvements, rather than to feel stymied or intruded upon. We can end up a captive of pride.

Soon, a woman from church she vaguely knew insisted on picking her up on Sunday mornings, since she only had to go a few blocks out of her way to do so. The conversations in the car there and back turned into unexpected gems. They found they both liked telling stories about their travels, and these tales led to their recounting adventures of the heart. They began lingering in front of her house after church with the motor off. Inviting her driver in for coffee followed, and this ritual became the ground of one of the deepest friendships of her life.

Discovery arises from formlessness, if we can withstand the uncertainty and go with the unexpected. Surfaces can be deceiving. Under normal circumstances, these two women would not have sought each other out, yet they had stumbled upon a rare fluency. Something exciting happens when we rid ourselves of our long-established ideas about how to live and who might be worth our time.

Introspection is a vital use for courage, but it may be the most belated. Many of us put off the work of self-examination as long as we can. Loved ones may complain of an emotional distance that shuts them out or a temper that shuts them down, but we defer searching for the causes that might suggest solutions. When we are not at our jobs, it is easier to sink into the oblivion of back-to-back entertainments and to use food or alcohol as additional narcotics. We assure ourselves that things are going well enough, until something happens that thrusts us into a necessary reckoning.

At fifty-one, a woman was promoted to the supervisory level at her workplace. Shortly after beginning the new position, she responded so harshly to a struggling employee that she was appalled by her own conduct:

> I crushed him, when all he needed was a nudge in the right direction. The look on his face stunned me. For years, my husband had been begging me to soften up, not to be so heavy-handed with the kids, with him. All of a sudden, I saw what he'd been trying to tell me. I don't know why, but then and there I really faced up to it for the first time.

This woman saw that she had long been ruled by a propensity to scold. Most jarring was the connection she made to herself as a girl cowering before her father's tirades. "He was relentless. Somehow I must have gotten the idea that this is what you do if you want to be respected. But it only makes you feared. I knew this intellectually, but I had finally applied it to myself."

She began a practice of pausing before she admonished anyone, at work or at home. When the impulse arose, she would visualize receiving her father's barbs. "That was the last time I ever let anyone have it like that," she said. "Thank God for getting old enough to face myself. I had considered myself an easygoing person. I just couldn't see what I was doing. But now that I see it, I am banishing it as an option."

Many of our flaws remain invisible until we accumulate enough strength to oppose them. In particular, self-deception about how well we treat others can persist in spite of all evidence to the contrary. Finally, the day may arrive when we notice how a particular problem has recurred in each of our relationships, or how people from disparate areas of our lives have had the same complaints. What had long been obvious to everyone else comes to us as a revelation.

Transformation is initially about inquiry more than answers, exploration rather than outcome. By tangling with the truth about ourselves, we can begin to make long-awaited progress in life. This woman needed to come to terms with how fragile her own self-respect was underneath her bluster. With hurt, disappointment, or any challenge to her authority, she went back to feeling like the powerless young girl she had once been. Finding the middle ground between scolding and crumbling was her true work, to which she applied herself with alacrity and with the many life skills she had acquired over the years. The awareness itself had given her a measure of mastery that she was able to employ as a starting point.

Initially, there is no way to blunt the humiliation of confronting such matters. We can only assure ourselves that missteps and faltering bespeak our humanity. While we grapple, loved ones who must contend someday with their own blunders watch how we take responsibility and permit ourselves to expand beyond our prior limits. Coming to grips with our weaknesses from the past is a valiant and ultimately liberating attainment.

A woman in her early sixties finally gave in to her husband's pleas to sell the sprawling house where they had raised their three children. He was eager to dispose of most of their possessions and move into a small apartment. She dreaded the idea of sorting through piles of papers, tossing out souvenirs of their travels, and parting with furniture that had accompanied them all of these years, especially an antique chest of drawers that had been given to her years ago by her grandmother.

During the process of throwing things

away, this woman felt as though she was undergoing a purging, a preparation for inner clarity such as a monk might undertake. "For the longest time, I thought I couldn't live without a house full of furniture and a thousand books. But each time we gave away a sofa or a carton of books, I felt lighter." Tossing out papers upon papers, she found that she missed none of that accumulation once it was gone. But her grandmother's chest of drawers remained a stumbling block.

Month after month, she found excuses for delaying the move. She accused herself of petty attachment and browbeat herself mercilessly, until she came to a realization: "The idea hit me that the chest had only been on loan to me — that it was time for my daughter to be the one watching over it. Suddenly, I could let go of it. I was even happy the day the moving truck came to take it to her house, along with boxes of items that she wanted from her childhood. I was free at last."

Relinquishment shows us the true contours of our courage. After they settled into their new quarters, she found that the feeling of lightness did not leave her. We think our identity hinges on living in a particular house with all of our things, and then one day we learn how little was necessary all along.

18
THE BODY'S LESSONS

Though much is taken, much abides . . .
ALFRED LORD TENNYSON

By the time we are in our fifties, we each must contend with some kind of physical deterioration. With inactivity, we lose muscle tone faster. We gain weight with the slightest nibble of a treat. We lose close vision, cope with pain in odd places, and watch our skin begin to hang. This is the essence of biology — time's inevitable encroachment — which we know down to our bones in our seventies, eighties, and nineties.

The body does not have to bring the spirit down with it. Dizziness from my inner ear keeps me from whirling with the polka, but I can soar in other ways when I waltz. I must restrict my intake of sodium, but my salt sensitivity has grown so acute that I enjoy trace amounts. Elders who endure far more restrictions have shown me inventive ways to live well in spite of physical constraints. For each faculty torn away, we must watch for a compensation and make sure we are alert to every capacity that abides.

I once knew a concert pianist whose hands were ruined by arthritis. After a year of mourning, she realized that she could hear the piano perfectly well in her mind. She would listen to several versions of the same piece, then devise her own interpretation for hours on end. When I visited her in the nursing home, I often came upon her tapping out the notes on the arm of her wheelchair, her face transfixed by what she was fashioning.

I was walking through an old-growth forest in Olympic National Park when I came upon a giant fir tree that had lost its top. All the branches that had once reached the sun above the forest canopy were gone, having snapped off in some kind of terrible gale. Amazingly, this aged Queen of the Forest had not died from the amputation. She had many tiny branches growing out of her rough, sturdy trunk, allowing her to gather the sun's nurturance down below. I saw that bits of dappled light were reaching this new growth, granting minimal photosynthesis — just enough to sustain her last years.

There is a certain point where we make our own fate. Elders who reach for life despite the ravages of frailty or illness are like this tree, extending their slender efforts with as much vigor as they can muster. They persist, even though they cannot get their full majesty back and they know it. They strive each day to affirm the privilege of still being here to receive that dappled light.

Every morning, when I was between the ages of eight and eighteen, I would watch an old man walk briskly by my bedroom window. If there was no school, I would also be able to see him returning a few hours later with a newspaper tucked under his arm. "He'll outlive all of us," my mother used to say, admiring the strength of his stride and his faithfulness to his morning routine. I was most intrigued by his face, full of wonder and appreciation, as if he had never seen the world before.

Years passed, and the old man kept on getting his newspaper this way through bitter winters and hot, humid summers. His pace slowed down a bit, but he was always out there. I imagined that it was lonely inside his house, otherwise why would someone trek two and a half miles each way to the store? My high school was across from that shopping center, so I came to know the meanderings of the route from my own bicycle rides. I found it too tedious to walk there and back.

Some elders do sit home immobilized, bemoaning their pain and stiffness. Their overfocus on the body becomes a vortex, pulling them down deeper as inactivity makes them weaker. Other elders are like my 84-year-old friend who swims every day at her local YWCA to keep her joints from aching. "This way, I don't have much pain and I hardly ever stiffen up." She exudes well-being, keeping her mind on matters other than arthritis.

"You have to put your mind to it," said a man in his early seventies, still fighting the aftereffects of a stroke he had suffered many years earlier. With half of his body barely functioning, he decided at the time to refuse a wheelchair and learn how to walk with a cane. It is still tricky for him to pull up his pants with one hand while balancing upright. He sometimes has to find someone in the hallway of his assisted-living residence to haul up his waistband a few more inches. "It's what I have to do." Having once been a mountain climber, he knows what it is to persevere.

Each time I see him, I am struck by this man's quality of presence. There is no sense of bemoaning his fate. He is proud of still being able to walk, relieved that his lifelong athletic abilities continue to serve him well. His eyes convey a resonant sensitivity and alertness. The healthy half of his body does double-duty, and his towering spirit keeps him whole.

As her body aged, a ballerina named Dominique Gabella was expected to give up dancing and make the transition to choreography and teaching. But dancing remained just as important to her as ever. She kept on. By the age of fifty-eight, she felt there was a depth to her performances that her earlier dancing had lacked. "When you are young, the soul does not speak in the same way."[1]

Lost capacities are a major source of grief in later life, but what the soul knows keeps enlarging. By adapting her movements to what her body could still handle, this ballerina was able to make use of conviction born of long-standing intent. Her legs could no longer reach as high, but there were things she knew at this point in her life that more than made up for technical insufficiency. Her audiences could feel this artistry, even if conveyed through a less-than-dazzling arabesque or a leap that did

240

not risk her fragile knees.

Acceptance of decreased ability is not the same as capitulation. When our customary way of functioning is blocked, we can either rage at what has been taken away or begin to open ourselves to new approaches. An artist who did precise pen-and-ink renderings in her youth and middle years developed a hand tremor that made her work increasingly difficult. As an elder, she switched to painting when it became clear that she had no other choice. "I was completely surprised by what I could do with broad brushstrokes, eruptions of color. It was all loose, unplanned — nothing like my tight compositions — yet certain skills carried over, and there were others I didn't know were in me."

A 71-year-old woman losing her central vision was devastated when her doctor informed her that her blindness would only worsen with time. An avid reader, she grieved hard and long. Then, she decided to hold a book give-away party. She invited all of her friends to come over and choose armloads of books to take home with them. She retained a single row of her most cherished books. To her surprise, three friends offered to visit weekly to read aloud to her. She began keeping three books going at a time, so that each reader could pick up where she left off.

One of her readers told me, "I look forward so much to these afternoons. It's the only time I stop rushing around. Plus, there's nothing like being immersed in a good novel with a friend." The weekly visits were animated by mutual pleasure and sweet intimacy, rather than mere utility. Reader and listener, giver and receiver, became indistinguishable. Many kinds of yearning were quenched.

When first facing a loss as profound as going blind, it is almost impossible to see the compensations that might be just around the bend. A few months into her new way of reading, this woman observed, "Something has been taken away, and something has been given." Her grief about her encroaching blindness still revives with each diminishment of her vision, but this sorrow has never overtaken her as it had initially. She celebrates the colors and shapes she still can see and the friends that make all the difference.

Aging is public. We can hide other facts about ourselves, but we carry time so visibly that everyone can see in a glance that we have left our youth behind. No matter how artfully a face has been adorned or hair has been colored, it is evident to all that an older person owns the altered visage. How we feel about the length of our chronology is therefore also on display, not only in our attempts at concealment but in a stance that bespeaks acceptance or resistance, pride or shame.

In my late forties, I remember watching with some bemusement as people in their fifties and older fumbled for their reading glasses or cursed when they could not see what I was trying to show them. *What a shame.* A few years later, when it started to happen to me, I was appalled. Somewhere out of my awareness I had managed to cultivate the idea that I was going to be exempt, that my eye muscles would manage to maintain their youthful elasticity — even if everyone else's did not. The body does not permit us to maintain the fiction of invincibility for long.

Asked about the secrets of her longevity, a centenarian mused about the importance of taking the changes as they come and melding oneself as best one can to each phase of living:

I realize I am always adapting to the next lesson in life. I have been old now for more than thirty years. I thought I was old at seventy, but then thirty more years have just flown away. I've had a lot of adapting to do with each decade. . . . I've kept changing my activities to fit my physical limitations. In my eighties I adapted to not going out as much as before. . . . I don't feel too different about being a hundred. After all, it's just a matter of good health and circumstance. I'm glad that I still have the use of my legs, my arms, my hands, my brain. I'm so thankful for common everyday health.[2]

I was puzzled when I first met a woman in her mid-eighties who never left her apartment, despite being in relatively good health. She explained: "Dear, a lady does not go out in public without her high heels." Her doctor had forbidden her to wear anything but flat shoes due to severe arthritis in her toes. To preserve her self-image along with her toes, she had rendered herself homebound.

We had it out. I countered that there must be other ways to feel ladylike than to perch on heels. I hated to think of her confined by the need to maintain appearances. She insisted that I had no idea what it was like to go out there feeling shabby and treated like a little old lady: "The young are so disparaging." Sadly, I pointed out that if she continued to staying home she would slowly lose her energetic stride and perhaps also her lively demeanor. We sat there, dead-locked, but neither of us would concede defeat.

The next time I visited, she held up a pair of fancy athletic shoes. I had successfully frightened her into taking daily spins around her neighborhood in her sturdy new shoes. "I feel like a truck driver," she said, "but I go at dawn, before the young wake up." There was no way she was going to forfeit her self-image to gain her mobility.

In the realm of the body, life does not get better for most of us, yet the most vibrant elders I have seen emanate self-acceptance in this respect. They show in their every gesture that they have come to be at ease in their own skin. A 63-year-old woman once surprised me by insisting that her life had gotten better on a physical level as she had gotten older:

In my younger years, I was dissatisfied with my body. I was always finding fault with it, and I was ashamed of its many flaws. Ever so slowly, I've come to accept my body as it is — its many imperfections and strengths. I don't dwell in judgment anymore. I wake up every morning and enjoy the body I have.

At sixty-five, the writer Susan Jacoby juxtaposed her worst-case scenarios and her hopes about getting older. Citing accomplished elders who had gone on contributing to their professions to the very end, she wrote:

> I, too, hope to go on being productive, writing long after the age when most people retire, in the twilight of the print culture that has nourished my life. . . . [But] it is chilling to think about becoming helpless in a society that affords only the most minimal support for those who can no longer care for themselves. So I must plan, as best I can, for the unthinkable. . . . What I expect . . . is nothing less than an unending struggle, ideally laced with moments of grace.[3]

We all fear a time when we cannot fend for ourselves. Our society's collective will falters in finding ways to provide for those with disabling conditions at any age. In observing individuals in these predicaments, however, I have seen a range of creative adaptations rather than unremitting bleakness. We cannot know until we arrive at that point what kind of life we may manage to patch together and who will participate in the inventive alliances we devise. We cannot imagine which of our capacities, unnoticed during times of health and independence, will become windfalls that help us live well in spite of limitations.

When I worry about the physical compromises that might befall me as I get older, I invoke the image of the old man who walked by my bedroom window every morning, how he kept on moving and gave himself a reliable rhythm around which to assemble his days. I think of the spirit for life that got him out of bed and into the world, rain or shine, and I know what I will try to do.

19
ATTITUDE

My experience is what I agree to
attend to.

WILLIAM JAMES

Where we invest our attention makes all the difference in the character of later life. We must deliberately avoid giving the body's deterioration our focus and refuse the hobbling stereotypes that creep into our perceptions. If we expect to dwindle, we will not oppose the shrinkage of our experience. It is easier to feel deprived than grateful, to tally up one's losses than to count one's blessings. Opening ourselves to countervailing experiences is an effort, while bemoaning one's fate is as automatic as sighing. Like a muscle, an appreciative attitude must be developed and kept in top form. When we turn our attention in a vivacious direction, we generate the gusto for all that life has to offer.

An 84-year-old artist ceased painting for sixteen months following her husband's cancer surgery. In the meantime, her heart started going in and out of chaotic rhythms. "I didn't need the doctors to tell me I was heartbroken." Then she heard about a painting class being held in a town twenty miles away, led by a painter of some renown regionally: "Just being with other artists, smelling the paint, has revived me. I know if I don't have fun, I'll get depressed. I have to continue to let the child in me have a good time. Now my head is full of paintings I want to do. My spirit has been sparked."

Shortly before he died at the age of one hundred, the poet Stanley Kunitz was asked by his young assistant how he had repeatedly managed to use the power of his mind to overcome obstacles. "I don't know, but that's been a principle all my life to do what I can and more. And it's amazing that if you believe in that there's almost nothing that stands in your way except your own restrictiveness."[1]

I once took a friend's 94-year-old grandfather on an outing. It had been years since he last walked in the University District where he had grown up. I parked on the main drag and we set out. Suddenly, he stopped in his tracks in front of a fast-food place. "The pharmacy! It's gone!" As a boy, he had spun on the stools of their soda fountain and picked out candy from the great barrels near the front door. The stones of the original structure were still there on either side of the plate-glass window, but nothing else remained of what he remembered.

He demanded that I take him home, immediately. I offered to take him to another neighborhood nearby, full of old houses that had been restored to their original dignity. He insisted on going straight home. Normally a gruff man, at this point he was growling, yet on the way home he told me how he used to walk over to the pharmacy clutching a penny, picturing which barrel lid he would lift for his treat of the day.

As he spoke, I tried on his outrage — this blasphemy — that a warm, personal emblem of his boyhood had been replaced by something blank and interchangeable. I was in my early thirties at the time. I was able to conceive of his grief for the pharmacy's vanishing, but why cheat himself of a walk? It seemed he was emphasizing what had been lost, while casting aside something within his grasp. We could have had a lovely time sauntering through one of Seattle's intact neighborhoods.

Occupying the aggrieved position can become an identity in itself. Misery is at least reliable. We can find a bit more bleakness every day to add to our supply, and then spend much of our time calculating our disproportionate share.

I dropped him back at the house he had bought seventy years earlier. It had once been the only house on the hill, with a view of the rolling fields of a dairy farm. The green expanse had been turned into a shopping mall with vast stretches of parking spots. He had lost a great deal, I mused, but he was lucky to be able to go on living in his house, still on his own, the mortgage paid off long ago. He could still see, walk, and remember in his mid-nineties. There continued to be people in his life who loved him. I wanted to shout, "Isn't something better than nothing?"

Now I am old enough to have my own outrage at vintage houses turned into box-like duplexes, charming old coffeehouses having lost out to the bland chains. I can understand wanting to retreat into a remembered world, wishing to protect one's memories of how things used to be. I can recast his refusal to engage in the current scene as a passionate kind of defiance. I already feel the seduction of closing the door on change. But I also see how a young visitor was spurned and how she never offered to take him on an outing again.

A woman in her mid-seventies experienced a gradual slide into poverty as inflation rendered her pension insufficient for paying her bills, even when combined with her Social Security income. She decided to take a job clearing and wiping down tables at a fast-food place a few blocks from where she lived. Work like this was far beneath her previous station in life, and it hurt her pride when she first put on the uniform of the minimum-wage worker.

From ten a.m. until two p.m. every day, she watched the human spectacle: mothers with small children giving themselves a change of scene, workmen covered with plaster dust taking a break, a few fellow elders evading loneliness with a newspaper and the company of others. She kept the place immaculate, scooping up stray French fries and cheese-stained wrappers within moments of their descent to the floor. She had always been a hard worker, and she liked to see the place looking tidy and the tables gleaming in the morning sun.

The rhythm of getting out of the house

four hours a day ended up serving her soul. Once she went out among people, she realized she had been too much alone. She had more energy after coming home from work, as compared to how tired she had been feeling without variety to her days. Here and there, she was giving bits of advice to her young co-workers who told her their troubles back by the trash cans. Their stories were outside of her life experience, yet something in her solidity made them seek her out.

She told me with some bemusement that she loves going to work. "My boss bows to me when I come on duty. I'm so much more reliable than the kids he has to put up with." Far from feeling demeaned, she now feels pride in a job well done. The overheard conversations are entertaining, and there are times when she strikes up lively conversations with customers like me who wonder what the heck she is doing there. Surveying the place with her broom and dustpan in hand, she has the bearing of a queen.

In later life, the internal climate we create for ourselves matters more than ever. We set the tone of our days through this dominance of thought over experience. Where we place our focus determines which aspects of life will become salient and which will recede in importance. We can make things worse for ourselves by passing up a chance for renewal that comes our way, or we can welcome an invitation to be taken out for a change of scene when we have been stuck too long at home. We can remind ourselves that we are not helpless in this matter of choosing to grab hold of opportunity. Rather than forfeiting our own agency, we can watch for ways to accentuate the joys in our midst and to participate avidly in any encounter.

Appreciating our good fortune sometimes comes as a swoon, a sudden recognition of how much we have been graced by life's richness. A psychologist recounted a memory of his father breaking down and crying "copiously" during a religious service. At twenty-two, he listened with great interest when his father was asked by the man leading the service what was happening for him. His father replied, "Sometimes you don't know just how lucky you are."[2]

In daily life, we may be unable to cut through the haze of all the things we take for granted. Such moments of clarity occur more often as we get older, since knowing what deserves appreciation is an attribute of long survival. The more suffering we have endured, the more we perceive the magnitude of what other people have given to us and what we have been spared of life's potential disasters. We are grateful for what we have learned from others and what we have gleaned on our own. We notice each act of thoughtfulness and the small victories of pleasure over hardship. A man dying at the age of eighty-nine was handed a glass of ice water as he lay in his hospital bed: "It's so lovely, it's as though God made it for me."

From the vantage point of later life, a man recalled an elder who had lit up his boyhood with her vibrancy. Her example had stayed with him for a lifetime:

She was the happiest person I ever knew. Yet hardship was no stranger to her. She had lost her husband years before, her income was very meager, and her eyesight was failing. But she brought up her children and remained joyful toward life. . . . How I loved to visit her apartment. It was filled with cats, fish, birds, turtles, and a dog named Ginger. Every child on the block had a personal interest in them and she loved to have the children in. One day I asked her: "How can you keep track of all these animals?" She smiled and said: "I love to care for living things. They are a constant reminder of the beauty of life."

She showed that love of life every night when she would sit on her porch and warmly greet everyone who passed by.[3]

Self-centeredness tends to be a source of considerable unhappiness. Those who talk more than listen, or make demands rather than negotiate, often find other people pulling back from them. When combined with insensitivity toward others' feelings and an excessively blunt style, this inability to listen coupled with inflexibility may result in a dearth of long-standing relationships. Everyone wants to be heard, to matter to someone else, to be liked — but trying to get such needs met through coercion rather than reciprocity does not work. Adult children may keep their distance, siblings may become estranged, and intimate partners may come and go.

My mother was afflicted with this burden. She regularly ran over other people's feelings with the weight of her own misery and anger. When I was a child, she would vent her fury at salesclerks in department stores so loudly that I would insert myself into rows of tightly packed dresses to hide until the tirade was over. She was capable of creating a spectacular scene at any time, at any place, in front of anyone, to the mortification of those who belonged to her.

At seventy-one, she tried in vain to find a new man. Her second husband had died, and she was living in a community with a preponderance of older women in the same situation. If an eligible man moved in, he was immediately swamped with invitations. One day a handsome 84-year-old man named Mel moved in a few doors down. He was grieving his wife of almost sixty years and was in no mood for the female onslaught. My mother would encounter him occasionally in the parking lot or the laundry room. They struck up a friendship in which she mostly listened to his sadness about his wife's death.

I knew from her tone on the phone that she had developed a serious crush. Outwardly, she was keeping it well contained. She knew he was relieved in her company not to be treated like prey. A few months later, when the condo association was about to hold a dinner dance, she told Mel he ought to let her introduce him to people. "It's time to come out of yourself," she urged. He accepted.

The night of the dance, she called lots of people over to their table within the first half hour. Mel was surprised to be enjoying himself. When the music began, he asked my mother to dance. She said, "No, you have to circulate. Put yourself out there. Live a little." She reminded him that she knew a lot about being widowed. Minutes later, a blood vessel burst in her brain. Her left hand, then her left leg and her entire left side became numb. She slumped over. "I'm having a stroke," she wept. Mel held her while they waited for the ambulance.

"She died being a mensch," Mel told me a few days later. When I went into her bedroom to face packing up her belongings, the perfume she had put on that night was still in the air. Makeup was strewn all over her bathroom counter. I cried over each of the seven dresses, still on the bed, that she had tried on like a teenager.

Everything about my mother is more vivid, now that her presence is not in the way. I can see her pleasure in finally putting her bitterness aside and doing right. Her spirit soared in coming out of herself. Everyone told me how beautiful she looked that night, how she was shining.

In the last third of our lives, living fully requires digging down into the capacities that have grown inside us while we were busy getting through youth and midlife. It may mean pushing aside old hurts so that we have more room for seeing others accurately. Having craved consideration and respect, we may decide to offer these qualities to those we know and extend our empathy further than ever before. It is possible thereby to stumble upon new ways of relating and fresh emotional territory. Putting our attention on others — emerging from a self-orientation — is a reliable path to contentment at any age, but such a shift in attitude later in life can become revelatory.

20
SLOWING DOWN

We have to slow down, because we do not have much time.

ZEN SAYING

To inhabit the moment in front of us more fully — it seems as though this should be a simple matter of deciding to do so, but our thoughts and anxieties distract us. Quieting the mind sufficiently is difficult. It is hard to stop hurrying mentally toward the next task, fretting about something in the future, or ruminating over something that happened the day before. Even if we vow not to squander the next hour through inattention, it happens. We slip back into our thoughts and forget to be awake.

We must repeatedly remind ourselves to pause, to slow down for as much aliveness as we can muster. By doing so, we reach an accord directly with time and obliquely with death. Otherwise, days run into each other without the distinction of our having paid attention, and we have the sense of hurtling swiftly toward the ending.

At the age of seventy-five, a retired psychiatrist took a fall in a dark parking lot that could have ended his life. He realized that he had come close to aging "fifty years in one fell swoop." In the aftermath, he wondered, "Could I defeat time by being more aware?" A heightened consciousness took hold of him: "I live on the cusp, savoring every moment, every hug and kiss from Katie, every chance to see my grown children, every friend, every sunset and cloud in the New Mexico sky, every interested student, every conscious second."[1]

In the last months of her life, my mother-in-law dwelled in a hospital bed in our house. It took all of her strength to get down our steep front steps, walk around the block, and get back up to the front door, but we did this together three or four times a week. As we inched down the sidewalk, she pointed out every flower, the pattern in paving stones, the various shades of green in the trees and bushes. I had never seen my neighborhood before — not like this — even though I had walked this circuit at least a thousand times with my dog. She noticed artful decorations on mailboxes, the way handrails had been constructed, the varieties of front doors, and had something to say about all of it.

At first, I was infuriated by the slowness of our pace. I had other things to do. She would stop often, not because she was short of breath, but out of the need to examine the texture of the petals of a flower or to get a closer look at the edging around a driveway. Gradually, I surrendered. There was no way to hurry a dying woman. I began to look forward to these walks. What else would we notice that we had not seen before? I let go of the concerns bombarding my mind and opened up to just seeing what was there.

Normally, it is hard to give ourselves even fifteen minutes of the day like this. Such alertness requires putting aside our preoccupation with what will happen later, tomorrow, and the day after that. It means overcoming the nagging distraction of our many pressures and aims. My mother-in-law reminded me of the patient momentum of looking and really seeing, turning an ordinary walk into gladness for continuing to be among the living. Long after she died, I would walk the neighborhood and challenge myself to walk like that, to be alive like that.

■ ■ ■ ■

During a walk around the neighborhood years later, I overheard a woman talking on her cell phone while she was planting some bulbs in her front yard. She said, "Yeah, I put my gardening time on my calendar. It's the only way I can get myself out here." I was rattled. The idea of scheduling gardening time, rather than simply going out to the garden, seemed to cancel out the joy of digging in the dirt. Also, she was not letting herself luxuriate in the experience of being outside, smelling the soil and the sweetness of the fresh air. Her attention was divided, barely there.

The forfeiture of immediacy is becoming more and more commonplace. We are supposed to accede to the fact that at any moment our actual presence may be discarded in favor of someone else's virtual presence. When a phone call or text message comes in from afar, another person's company is no longer considered sacrosanct.

A 71-year-old grandmother described the rules she implements when giving her teenaged granddaughter rides anywhere:

Everything is off, even the car radio. You

want a ride? You have to talk to me. No thumbs flying on those little gadgets, nothing stuck in your ears — you're with Grandma and nobody else. Keeping your face in some screen when we could be together — I won't have it. I stopped driving on the freeway, so she's stuck in the car with me longer with all those traffic lights and side roads. Funny thing is, she's not complaining. She yaks to me like my kids used to. We're having us a good time. I'll be sad when she gets her driver's license next year and I won't be able to trap her anymore.

Communication is now so constant, we can barely stand it. We have trouble clearing the mental space to listen fully to each other or engage wholeheartedly in a solitary pursuit. Half-listening with a distracted mind has become acceptable. Every waking moment, we are being entertained and informed, getting things done, or engaging in stilted electronic contact. We rarely grant ourselves the distinct peacefulness of doing only one thing at a time or giving one person absolute primacy.

We do not nurture our relationships well or fully engage our creativity in time slots. Hearts open and artistry unfolds in a state of flow, when we are not keeping track of time or letting it matter. A conversation or an idea can proceed in any direction, according to the whim of circumstance. A poem, a painting, or a story — each benefits when we dispense with constraints on our spontaneity. Once we allow the free play of emotions, letting thoughts and images drift, some of our best intimacy and inventiveness may arise.

A woman recalled sitting on her grandmother's bed as a child and listening to her tell a story prompted by each item they had taken out of her jewelry box. Suddenly her mother was standing in the doorway, having caught them in this mutual enchantment. After she scolded them for "daydreaming" and left, her grandmother explained:

> Your mother goes and goes and does and does, but she never considers who she is. It is too bad she never stops to treasure anything or make anything special. She thinks that I am moaning because I am sick and that is true. Soon I will die, but I am also calling. I am calling and wooing out my memories, all the special moments, all the moments when dreams met with life and came true.[2]

An 86-year-old woman volunteered at the day-care center for the children of her retirement community's staff. She told me that the hours she spent there, holding children on her lap during nap time, were better than anything on her facility's activity calendar. "When a child falls asleep in my arms, sometimes I breathe in unison and go into that wonderful peace myself. I don't mean I fall asleep. I am awake — really awake — and listening to what's going on around me, but I am in some other sphere. It's terrific. They should charge for it."

In later life, physical circumstances may grant us the necessity of reclaiming a more simplified pace. We may be unable to do three things at once. With compromised mobility, we may again find reverence being in another's company and giving our wholehearted focus. We may have no choice but to occupy the kind of time where vibrancy is located.

I have a friend in her early eighties who must focus her daily energy carefully, because she has so little of it. When she folds her laundry, she is folding her laundry. She props herself up against her dryer while her hands are engaged, hoping her unsteady legs will support her long enough to get the job done. She sets her cell phone beside the pile of laundry in case there is a call, but if she is summoned she picks up the phone and puts down her laundry. Concentrating on the call is all she can do, she told me with a laugh, lest she fall over.

When I call her, I know I have her full attention. She conveys the feeling that there is nothing more important she could be doing at that moment. The pleasure of our time together on the phone has far more centrality than when I am talking with the breathless young, caught up in their pressures and barely able to sustain their attention to the end of a sentence.

A woman living in a nursing home asked me to retrieve a poem she had written from the corkboard on her wall. There it was, tacked up between the nursing home's calendar of events and the menu for the month. A few weeks earlier, she had woken up one morning with the poem already half born. Laboriously, she scribbled the lines onto a napkin with her stroke-destroyed scrawl. She worked on the poem throughout the day, changing a word here and there, and then got up the courage to read the finished version to the cheers of her tablemates at dinner.

I handed her the napkin. She read the

poem out loud to me, slowly, savoring the rhythm of each line. I took a deep breath and put aside my sense of hurry, shutting out all the tasks awaiting my attention. The tree outside her window was her inspiration. I turned to look at it and settled into the sweetness of what was being conveyed. The entirety of nature had come to be compressed in this one tree and the portion of sky visible behind it. Her words lingered on the subtle changes in the angles of light on the branches. I felt as though I had been taken inside her gaze to the hundred mornings she had watched this light. When she finished, we let a few moments hang in the air around the poem, and then she asked me to tack it back up between the calendar and the menu.

Inwardly, in the territory of the soul, there is no disability. In many ways, this woman's capacity to delve into poetry's domain had been enabled by her stroke. She had been simultaneously restricted and freed by becoming half paralyzed. She told me that there had been so much more silence in her life since she had been "struck down" and that the poem seemed to arise out of that silence. In her late eighties, she did not worry whether or not she was a poet. Her poem declared itself, and so did she.

She refused my offer to type it up on fancy paper, preferring to keep the frayed napkin with her own handwriting in her line of sight. She liked that it was on a napkin and that the words she had discarded were still visible. "You can see how it came straight from my heart." Anyone who came into the room to help her get dressed had to reckon with a woman who wrote poetry.

Throughout midlife, we suffer from a shortage of open time. What we most crave is a span without commitments, an oceanic interlude without boundaries. Once adolescence ends, gone are Saturdays given over to making up songs on the guitar or getting lost for days in an 800-page novel. Most of us only get this during designated periods made vacant of tasks and commitments. They're called vacations.

As elders, we reach a phase in life when hurrying may at last subside. When we start slowing down and doing less, more life becomes available to be experienced and remembered. We can cease mulling over the past or projecting ourselves into the future, at least for a moment or two between onrushing thoughts. With a singular focus, we let things come as they will and feel the wonder of the sensate world, the here and now, where peace resides.

At the age of seventy-one, a woman contrasted the frenetic pace of her younger years with the serenity of her current life: "I was so scattered. I was focusing on my children, on my work as a teacher, taking care of everything. I was running around all the time, barely keeping up. I was responsible for so many things. Now I can meditate. I am grounded. I can undertake something and stick with it. There's really no comparison."

By refusing the insistence of haste, we expand the hours in front of us. Sitting still and reflecting becomes a bold reply to evanescence, a kind of grabbing hold. By reveling in what has been seen and heard and felt, we may find that time finally attains a pace that feels like living.

21
COMPOSURE

That which youth found and had to find outside the self, in the second half of life must be found within.

CARL JUNG

By the time we reach later life, we have taken on and discarded so many self-conceptions that we are well familiar with their gossamer qualities. We have less tolerance for decorative surfaces, the trappings donned in order to get ahead, fit in, or be liked. Where once we may have needed these props of identity and status to tell us who we were, now we care only about what is most individually rewarding or essential. Having other people support our stance is affirming, but is no longer necessary. This is the great discovery of individuality.

A man in his fifties marveled at how far he had come since the formlessness and insecurity of his youth:

There are so many things I used to put up with when I was younger. I would tolerate situations I hated for the longest time. I don't think I even recognized when I was miserable — in relationships, at work, whatever. Now, I pay attention to how I'm feeling, how I'm reacting. I respect my own sense of what's going on. I don't force myself to take it. If things aren't right for me, I know it and I get the heck out of the situation. I'm getting better and better at this.

An unflappable inner stance is often the sweet fruit of decades of living. This does not mean the cessation of all doubt, but rather taking uncertainty in stride. We still get upset, but rarely does upheaval stir us to the core. Our equanimity has grown large enough to dwarf our smaller disappointments. We know we are not invincible, but we are more certain about the aspects of ourselves that have been tested over time. We are more determined than ever to live well, to break through the limits of our anxieties and get on with the business of flourishing.

An old friend once supplied a few evocative details and catapulted us both back to the poignant period after we had graduated from college, when we had no idea what to do with our lives. It seemed everyone else was following a well-considered path, like graduate school, a trip around the world, or a position in their family's company. We were among the lost, and it was awful.

We recalled using white paper plates to sketch out the parameters of our indecision. We both filled in our options in neat pie slices radiating out from the center. We had nothing linear to go by, no set sequences or plans to anchor us, only a dizzying fate that could be spun around like a roulette wheel. The pointer could land anywhere. We spent hours rotating our respective plates and imagining each section as it might or might not be lived out, wondering which direction would be best and how we were supposed to decide.

Recounting those tortured afternoons with our paper plates, we laughed and cried together. It was almost thirty years later, and we had gone on to live out possibilities that had not even merited a slice on our circle of options. Somehow we had moved from that amorphous state to becoming women in our fifties with full and satisfying lives. We recognized in ourselves intimations of the young women we had once been, at the same time that we realized how little of our current lives could have been predicted back then.

These remembrances with my friend made it possible for me to reclaim a part of myself that I had never fully understood. I felt like a wise old aunt bringing succor and reassurance to my previous self, even admiring her for venturing out into the world without a master plan. That 22-year-old wanderer was determined to be true to herself, even if this meant suffering the ache of nonconformity and living for a while without a dime to her name.

Along the way, fundamental ideas about how I saw the world became the core beliefs that anchored me. Later, when I had to make decisions, I assessed my course of action in terms of whether or not it violated those beliefs. My standpoint was no longer subject to such alarming drift. I had evolved a sense of myself, a mix derived from my experiences and all I had learned from others. At last I had developed my own perceptions, my own slant.

It can take a lot of living before we get to reside comfortably in our individuality. We all have influences we must throw off and those we need to absorb. One experience teaches us what we value in life, another shows us what we disdain. As the years pass, what we consider praiseworthy changes. Most of us become more interested in people's conduct than their status, their character more than their attainments. Acting decently becomes the basis for our self-respect, as well as how we judge others. Gradually, integrity comes to speak for itself.

A few summers ago, I invited a young woman from a neighboring campsite to join us for our humble campground repast. We sat at a picnic table amidst tall cedar and pine trees, in the foothills of the Olympic Mountains, and talked about life. She was searching for a sense of direction, traveling by herself in order to hear her own thoughts. She had just graduated from college a few months before and was feeling as lost as I had so many years earlier. I applauded her for making her own way and daring to seek her own answers, telling her the story of the paper plates and assuring her that it would all work out.

On the way to finding our own voice, we come to see that the deepest influences are the hardest to recognize. We may mistake inherited convictions for reality and familial attitudes for truths, naturally overlooking that which contradicts them. Ways of seeing the world and experiencing life tend to persist quietly in families, reverberating from one generation to another. We may not be aware of these assumptions because they come to us wrapped in the certainty of received beliefs. We surmise that this is how we are supposed to live.

A woman in her early sixties realized her mother's anxieties had dominated her far too long. She was determined to unleash herself:

I always had to be doing something. I felt like I ran from worry to worry. It was as though my mother was living inside me, but it took me a long time to see this. When I turned sixty, I decided I wasn't going to live this way anymore. I was going to take it easy, at least once in a while, hopefully a little bit more every day. It was time to leave open spaces on my calendar, not filling in each and every moment with tasks and commitments. It has taken me a while to get used to this. Part of me still panics when there's too big of a blank space. But it's getting easier.

Her mother had immigrated to this country knowing no English and had to work all the time to make ends meet. She raised her children with a stern austerity that left little room for play or joy. Gradually, the daughter was liberating herself from the generational constraint on her spirit. "I know I was kind of a taskmaster with my own kids — not as bad as my mother, but I did pass it on. I can see the relief in their faces when they catch me relaxing." She knew the time had come to live her own story.

To recognize an intergenerational theme like this is to begin to break free of it. We can then identify the ways we have carried it forward or see how we may have granted it too much sway by trying too hard to oppose it. Learning to heed our inner promptings means neither acceding to external influences nor rebelling against them, but rather permitting periods of repose when we can discern our own thoughts and feelings. Listening to what arises when we ponder our reactions is the surest means for finding a stance we can call our own.

A man in his early sixties recalled how cruel words spoken by his father on his deathbed had constricted his life from his twenties onward, until he managed to extricate himself years later:

Right before he died, my father told me

that I was a nothing and that everything I did would come to nothing. He was furious that I refused to learn a trade and instead was going to graduate school to study something as useless as philosophy. I never did get my doctorate, but I've made my own way. It wasn't until my fifties that his voice inside my head started fading out. By the time I turned sixty, his voice was completely gone. Failure isn't a category of my experience anymore. This is such a liberation for me. I don't second-guess myself. I just live.

This man was finally living in a way that was in sync with himself. He had literally become self-possessed. He was calmer than he had ever been, approaching problems with a poise that would have been unthinkable previously. Where career decisions had always sent him into a tailspin, he was able to weigh the pros and cons of his choices in a reasoned and nuanced way. Even his posture was straighter. He was no longer trying to refute his father's condemnation, but rather living in accordance with his own standards. A sense of inner authority had developed slowly, but it had become clear.

When we are young, it is difficult to live on

our own terms. We neither know for certain what those terms are nor how we would enact them if we could name them. We simply cannot see much beyond the exigencies and pleasures of the present. We are afflicted with shortsightedness, just when we would most benefit from transcendence. Our field of vision is occupied by all that presses in on us.

We spend a large swath of our youth learning how to bear disappointment. When we are turned down for a job we badly wanted, we may get near to despair. Living off of savings, sending out résumés like missives into the void, eating cornflakes for breakfast, lunch, and dinner — we fear failure everywhere we turn. Then the call comes and the siege is over. Paychecks return, and the new job leads us in fresh directions.

The first time a lover discards us becomes an aching loss that fills the whole world. For a while, we are unable to muster enthusiasm for anything. Once we manage to put ourselves back together, the memory of having done so is there for us the next time we are devastated. We become more assured that time is our ally and that unexpected vistas will open when the hurt eventually recedes.

As we enter midlife, pressures to prove

ourselves often persist as self-doubts. We may fret about not succeeding financially, not doing well enough at work, not being as accomplished as those we admire. In the personal sphere, we may worry about making mistakes, staying too long with the wrong partner, losing friends through inattention or a gradual drifting away. It takes years to quash insecurities like these and to develop a sustaining self-definition. Meanwhile, our fund of knowledge keeps broadening with the lessons from mistakes and the occasional luck of getting things right.

In a roundabout way, we gather up the vital elements of who we have been and all we have endured. At age one hundred and two, Mona Breckner was asked if she was still gaining wisdom and becoming more proficient at living at this point in her life:

Well, I'm not so much learning anything new, but I'm learning how to use the things that maybe I never developed before. And when I meet a situation that I don't quite know what to do with, I go through my experience and ask myself, Did I ever deal with anything like this before and was I successful? And I review in my mind the technique that I used and I think, Well, yes, this is something I've learned and can do again and again if the occasion demands it.[1]

Gradually, we may be able to accept our errors from the past without aching over them. Having developed an internal gauge of satisfaction, we begin to dispense with other people's judgments. We find our insecurities are not so vexing. We endure them and come out the other side. We lose one relationship and find another. We fumble financially and recover. Friendships go through periods of decline and renewal. A few of our youthful dreams are fulfilled and others are not, but the disappointment diminishes. We endure multiple insults to our desires, while finding that some of our most coveted accomplishments lose their luster once attained. Later, when we survey our life course, we often see how much better off we are than if fate had granted our original intentions.

Nearing sixty, a woman looked back on four decades of second-guessing herself and finding fault with her circumstances: "Wanting something to be different than what it is — a losing proposition for sure — but that's how I lived for years and years. I used to be strategizing all the time, trying to figure out what I was going to do. My mind was always on my next move."

She had come from a highly accomplished family, and her siblings had maintained careers commensurate with such expectations. At this point, she was running a neighborhood preschool program that had a long waiting list and enthusiastic parental support. Her modest house was paid off and she was able to live decently on the income from the school. "A few years ago, I took a look at my life and decided it was good enough. I don't wonder where I'm heading anymore. I tell myself today is what matters. I might as well make the most of what's right in front of me."

Pushing against adversity, we may be surprised by the grit we have acquired over the years. The upheavals of later life may reveal that our capacities are greater than we ever suspected. A woman nearing sixty-two had spent more than forty years going along with the dictates of her strong-willed husband. After his sudden death, a deluge of emptiness merged with her grief, but she had no time to drown:

Someone had to take over his business. I was a wreck, yet there I was making all those decisions. Just trying to figure out how he kept the books drove me crazy.

But it was good for me. I had so much to do every day, so much pressure, I had to function. The months went by and I started to have some confidence in myself. I was using my own mind. I always thought I'd be nothing without him, but I was feeling more solid than I ever had. It's been two years now, and I'm a changed person. I used to accept whatever was handed to me. Well, those days are over. I ask questions, I think for myself. I go with my gut, whatever feels right to me. This has been a long time coming. I feel as though I am coming into my own.

In my early twenties, I remember admiring people who had opinions, who could put forth their ideas with assurance and verve. I wondered where such firm judgments came from. I could be swayed from one view to another, depending on how fervently the points on one side or another were argued. It seemed there was a full spectrum of possible stances, many of them worthy. How was I to select among them? Who was I to judge?

Gradually, I realized that a great deal of posturing was going on, along with outright bluffing. It was easy to issue declarations unsupported by reasoning, to make arbitrary assertions based on a bad mood turned hastily into words. Alternatively, I saw that each of us has a particular take on a situation that may or may not be useful to someone else. No special prescience was necessary to hold a point of view, nor was anyone entitled to claim a superior vision merely on the basis of feeling convinced.

A 52-year-old woman said it had taken her years to feel like she had valid opinions and to be able to assert them:

> For more than twenty years, I attended my departmental meetings each week, but never said a word. It just took me a long time to believe that my take on things was worth inserting into the conversation. Now, when I have something useful to say, I say it. It helps that these days I'm not the only woman at the table, but mostly I think I have found my voice in getting older. They actually fall silent — all of them — whenever I speak. It turns out I have a lot of clout.

As we get older, we may become aware of having found a moral compass or a core of deep-seated attitudes. This internal reference point may form the basis for a welcome sense of composure. At last, we may be at ease with our convictions, as well as the array of aversions and sensitivities that our own truth comprises. The possibility of contentment grows inside us all along, but in later life we know how to hold it close.

22
BEGINNER'S MIND

In the beginner's mind there are many possibilities; in the expert's mind there are few.

SHUNRYU SUZUKI

When we are young, we regard elders as fixed in their ways. Then, as we get older, we start to notice how encased we had been in our earlier assumptions and expectations. The more we open ourselves to outside influences, the more we recognize just how limited our previous views had been. Much of what we long regarded as fact may be revealed to be merely our opinion, and we may see how we have nourished subtle prejudices with our ignorance. Our preconceptions tend to get routed out of us one by one.

In his eighties, Jung articulated later life's liberating mix of certainty and doubt, of knowing so much and so little at the same time:

> I am astonished, disappointed, pleased with myself. I am distressed, depressed, rapturous. I am all these things at once, and cannot add up the sum. I am incapable of determining ultimate worth or worthlessness; I have no judgment about myself and my life. There is nothing I am quite sure about.[1]

Eventually, we may see what it really means to have an open mind. We may dare to push aside the boundaries that have contained us and find out as much as we can beyond our customary sphere. We may feel less certain than ever about what we thought we knew, but more receptive to what it is possible to know. This is the start of true knowledge. A woman in her late fifties observed, "I realize I just have one slice of what there is to know. I don't have all 360 degrees. I've gotten more aware of the limits of this slice, and more interested in what's outside of it."

In fourth grade I longed to play the cello, but I chose viola because I could hide it under my coat on the way to school. Relentless ridicule was visited upon those in orchestra, and I knew I could not bear it. Year after year, I sat in rehearsals and envied the cellists beside me as we prepared for school concerts. Finally, I abandoned viola in the miasma of entering ninth grade. Just before my fifty-first birthday, I went out one day and bought a cello. Then I found a teacher willing to endure a stubborn adult, and now I have attained a decent vibrato and can play one of the slow movements of a Bach cello suite reasonably well.

I refuse to practice; I only play for pleasure. I might work on a tough section here and there, trying to improve, but generally I ask myself only to feel the instrument against my chest and to let the resonance of the sound move through me. Making time to play amidst a flood of other commitments, over and over again, proclaims the sweetness of satisfying a long-held desire. I have erased my former cowardice and given myself a lingering victory.

To gratify one yearning is to raise the hope that others might be fulfilled. The following summer, I decided to build a tree house. Ostensibly, it was to be for my grandchildren, but I pictured curling up with a book and a cup of coffee out there amidst the treetops or writing in my journal while listening to birdsong. I knew nothing about building — how to construct the walls, put in a floor, insert a window, hang the rafters, nail in shingles. My husband bought me an electric screwdriver, but otherwise pleaded ignorance as far as giving me further assistance.

Each time I went to the building-supply store, I would pick up vital tips as well as wood, screws, and brackets. Fellow customers — all of them men — took pity on me and sketched out ideas on the back of envelopes, giving me mini-lessons on how ends might be joined and corners reinforced. A 96-year-old retired builder in one of my elder groups coached me all the way through, particularly about safety with ladders. "If you feel queasy about reaching over to pound in that last nail, don't do it. Get down and move the ladder." Every week he grilled me on my adherence to this precaution. I am sure that he saved my life.

I did not lose my fear of the table saw, but I became good with a hammer and precise with a measuring tape. I loved loading up my carpenter's belt in the morning with my implements, every section holding something I would need while perched up high. When the window fit into the space I had prepared, I let out a shriek of joy. Blood was drawn by errant nails, mosquito attacks were endured, a hammer went flying off into the bushes, but I never broke my neck falling from the ladder. I built a little house in the forest where I play school with my granddaughters when they visit and where I have idyllic interludes by myself in all seasons.

Another piece of the world has become visible to me. I comprehend structures and appreciate building materials like never before. I walk by construction sites and examine the framing, how solidly beams are installed, and how well a roof is supported. I know what I am seeing. I attend concerts and watch how the cellist holds the bow, how the vibrato is delivered, and how the cellist's body adds animation to the tones. I know what I am hearing. I have the curiosity of the novice, just enough knowledge to drive the quest for more. The tree house and the cello make me wonder what else is next for me, how else I can expand.

Initially, to risk being a beginner again in later life is unnerving. Over the years, we become accustomed to striding into familiar undertakings with confidence. It has been a long time since we risked the tiny faltering steps of being new at something. Taking on this position, I feel vulnerable and ungrounded, as well as enlivened to a surprising degree. At cello recitals, I tremble while almost all of the children perform with aplomb, but the high afterward is extraordinary for my having stepped out into the galaxy of new learning.

A retired physicist attended an adult day center after a stroke put him in a wheelchair, half paralyzed. He looked askance when a sheet of paper was set out before him and a paintbrush was put into his good hand. "I don't paint," he scoffed, pushing the materials away. Meanwhile, the five other people at the table entered the swoon of creativity.

I watched him with my peripheral vision. I knew he detested being at the day center, being among the helpless. He looked around with scorn during the engaged silence. A woman seated next to him, with her stroke arm in a sling that kept getting in her way, was vigorously covering her paper with the semblance of leaves and flowers. A man across from him with the bewildered gaze of Alzheimer's was being drawn by his patchwork of lines into a place where memory loss did not matter. With nothing else to do, the physicist finally picked up a brush, moistened it with water, rubbed it vigorously on the nearest paint, and splashed a wave of bright red across the page.

He stared at the page, startled by the sight of that which his brush had declared. Then he amplified the red with a neighboring purple, and boldly blackened a section of the page to anchor what he had done. The effect culminated in a painting of arresting beauty, accomplished in less than a minute. He put the brush down, taken aback by his creation, as though it had been done by someone else.

This man became one of the most avid participants in the painting class. Week after week, he would be the first to set up his materials and the last to clean up. His work was soon featured in note cards sold by the day center for their fundraising. At the day center's annual art show, his paintings were snapped up before anyone else's and several advance requests for his work were submitted. All along, he regarded his surge of talent as an unexplained anomaly such as the universe frequently produces.

Many of us abandon our creative impulses as soon as we shed childhood's exuberance. Doing art for its own sake, the way a young child becomes immersed in the spontaneous glory of line and color, is gone. Boxed in by adult constraints, we rarely allow ourselves to venture beyond our routines and responsibilities.

Living long softens us and opens us up. Involvements formerly consigned to the bin of useless pursuits may become enthusiasms. Physical diminishment, in particular, demands a willingness to stretch ourselves and improvise. Just as nature abhors a vacuum, inventiveness becomes all the more necessary in stripped-down circumstances. With mobility compromised and time at loose ends, we may face the absolute ground of creativity — the need to make something out of nothing.

Following abdominal surgery, I was flat on my back for a month. I was in my early forties, in the midst of commitments from all directions that had to be halted. My surgery thus granted me an expanse of time. I took out a set of colored pencils that had gotten buried in the back of my desk for almost twenty years, unused. I had always intended to decorate the title pages of each of my journals, but there had been no time for such idle ornamentation. I drew entwining vines draped with tiny leaves along the edges of many pages. I watched the lovely sharpened point of my Spring Green pencil fill each leaf shape without a single smudge veering out of line. I twirled my hand-sharpener patiently, like the little girl I had once been, and let the shavings drop wherever they did. This was bliss.

A woman in her early fifties gave up her corporate career in order to devote herself to painting. She took a part-time job that paid a tenth of what she was accustomed to earning, but it gave her just enough to pay the rent in an artists' cooperative. Most important, it came with none of the stress that had previously left her in a continual state of exhaustion. She was ready to live what she considered her authentic life.

Once the commotion of the move settled down, she fell into an unproductive void. She stared at the blank canvas and self-doubt overwhelmed her. She was ripping through her savings at an alarming rate, going out to dinner, taking trips to visit friends, buying new clothes befitting her previous level of income. She realized that she had changed her circumstances but not her way of life. "Receptivity can't be turned on like a faucet. I realized I was trying to do art the way I had written procedure manuals — cerebral command and control. I needed to live differently, first of all."

She made a fresh start by yielding to her circumstances. She put herself on a strict budget better suited to her situation. Making her meals at home meant she had to locate herself within the simple rhythms of procuring and preparing food. Staying put on the weekends forced her to become more comfortable with her own company. Even shopping at thrift stores awakened her to the fun of serendipity, the random adventure of the treasure hunt. Overall, she relaxed her grip on how her days proceeded, taking long walks with her sketchpad in hand. Ideas for paintings began to come to her at odd moments, and she let these images guide her back to the canvas with new abandon.

A receptive mind is a triumph over complication. Throughout midlife, much that is unnecessary crowds in and takes up residence in our perception. We become so distracted that we miss out on the simplicity of seeing what is there. Daily life needs no adornment and suffers when too much is overlaid. Ordinary moments are sufficiently extraordinary, if we pay attention.

A few years into this phase of her life, she noted how her thinking and experiencing had been evolving: "I feel as though I am being opened up. My quality of mind is more holistic. I have a larger scope. It seems as if my emotional awareness has gotten more astute, like I read other people's feelings more easily. I'm sure it comes from going back to that creative space again and again. I have to keep going to the ground of myself in order to paint, and this has affected my relationships and the way I live."

Last year, I took a hike alone on a trail high above a rocky shoreline. The trail narrowed and became more and more treacherous. It was late December and no one knew I had set out on this particular trail that wintry afternoon. It occurred to me that if I slipped on one of the mossy outcroppings and fell, injuring myself just enough to be unable to walk, I would freeze to death out there before anyone looked for me. My level of alertness peaked with the sense of peril. I became attuned to the utter silence of the woods around me. I watched the placement of each step and took care to secure solid handholds for the worst of the craggy sections. When something vital is at stake, our sensitivity heightens and rewards us with fresh perceptions.

Stepping out into the void, finding new ways to live, is not easy. Long-established habits of thought and action fall away, replaced by levels of attentiveness and vigilance to which we may be unaccustomed. A woman in her mid-sixties described how the disparate eras of her past have combined to shape her in surprising ways:

> This business of getting older is so much more interesting and complicated than I could have ever suspected or even believed. The person I was in my twenties and thirties, some of the things I allowed to weigh me down then, I get to call silly now. But just as much, my earlier selves get to shake up anything rigid about how I live now. I had no idea back then that I would become such a mishmash of selves, with so many layers. Nothing is straightforward, and I keep on making discoveries.

It may become apparent that we have unexplored sides of ourselves, as do the people we love. We may reach the point where we are ready to gamble with our pride, to relax into inventiveness and go wherever this takes us. Vivaciousness in later life arises from a sense of wonder that has been set free.

23
THE HEART'S DESIRE

It is not difficult to be bold when one is young. The finest audacity is that of the end of life.

ANDRÉ GIDE

For years, everything and everyone seem to conspire to keep us from exploring what we really want to do. There are a thousand ways to numb ourselves to the urges that would shake things up. Family members' needs sap our energy; financial circumstances fence us in. Sitting down at the computer "just to finish up" a project from work easily turns into yet another evening or weekend lost to the job. Movies, television shows, and wandering through cyberspace can fill our nonwork time, until we are enveloped by passivity. *Next year,* we pledge to ourselves, only to let a few more years go by.

When his youngest daughter finished college, a 52-year-old electrician decided the time had come for a major change:

> Keeping up with the bills, giving my children — this is what I've been doing for more than twenty-five years. I told my wife, "Get ready to be poor" because fixing people's sockets and installing their lighting fixtures is going to be only a few days a week. The rest is for me, for figuring out the rest of my life. I'm ready now, even if it means watching my pennies.

The shock of realizing we have gotten older often turns *someday* into *now*. We suddenly locate ourselves further on the trajectory between birth and death, and a bolder spirit overtakes us. Whether a milestone in the lives of our children, a friend's heart attack, or the death of a parent who had seemed invincible, something spurs us to recognize that our former purposes do not suffice and we cannot wait any longer to follow our heart's desire.

I once labored in a painting class for a year, working on canvases as large as three by four feet. At first, the teacher gave us assignments I found overly prescriptive, e.g., "Use only two colors, plus black and white for shading." As the class advanced, he issued fewer directives. Soon, there was no starting point at all, no limits to hide within. It was awful. I would face the great blank expanse in front of me, afraid of committing myself with that first brushstroke. There were too many choices, too much open space to figure out. "Just sit with it," he urged. "See what comes." This waiting and listening, accepting an interlude of emptiness, proved to be both the hardest and the best aspect of learning how to make a painting.

Later life can feel like this, the more we dispense with externally imposed scripts. As we get older, we sit with tough questions: What do I want to accomplish before I die? What should I do with my remaining time? How can I live richly? These questions set off a period of reckoning. We are all too aware that an illness or accident might deprive us of the opportunity to enact our long-held passions.

A nursing home administrator in his mid-forties described a practice of walking through the corridors when he arrived each morning. He would find a staff person or a resident at random with whom to chat for ten or fifteen minutes, before he got involved in his budgets and memos. Seeing his workplace through the eyes of his employees and those who lived there highlighted the purpose of what he did the rest of the day. "Suddenly, back in my office, the day's tasks became meaningful rather than onerous. If something had gotten me stuck the day before, my morning chat usually threw it into perspective. I was off and running."

Seeing the ordinary from new angles quickens the pulse. Otherwise, we just live mechanically from one day to another, getting things done but not resonating with what we are doing. This administrator was awakening himself and his employees by hearing points of view that would not have been voiced in the usual round of meetings. The spontaneous and sincere nature of his inquiry brought out issues that needed to be addressed, as well as previously invisible victories that warranted the respect of his interest.

What we glean from hearing other people's stories and witnessing their triumphs energizes us. On subterranean levels, yearnings begin to stir in us as we listen to other people's hopes and desires. The legitimacy we grant others animates our own longings.

Through this practice of listening, the administrator decided to take a year's leave of absence to be a stay-at-home dad. After just a few months at home with his young sons, he found that immersing himself in their lives made him happy in a way that running the nursing home had not. He officially resigned from the post for good. Fortunately, his wife was pleased to return to her former workplace, and both were ready to adapt to living on a different scale financially.

This man had never considered child-rearing as a valid masculine occupation. He had grown up believing only activities that earned a living and enabled him to be a provider were acceptable. To broaden our exploration, we often have to clear away prior self-definitions and even the constructs we use for assigning value. This is how freedom begins. We have to dare to venture beyond the familiar landmarks of identity in order to locate the next version of ourselves.

A woman in her late forties realized she had spent most of her life living up to her family role as "the helpful one." Since childhood, she had always been the one to lift up family members in distress. Over the years, this pattern had naturally extended into her workplace. Colleagues expected her to jump to their aid when bidden, and she responded reflexively. Gradually, this way of being had become central to her identity.

At midlife, she reached the point where she was determined to make room for her own needs. How much of herself could she stop giving away without feeling selfish? Rather than repudiate her decency, she resolved to find less excessive ways to be generous with both family members and colleagues. She hoped to come up with new responses to anyone who depended on her more than was necessary. Entering a period of introspection, she began examining how she conducted each of her relationships, including her marriage of more than twenty years.

She discovered right away that her first reflex was to scan for what others wanted from her, even before they asked, and without checking within herself for her own preferences. She decided to try saying "no" in situations where she would previously have said an automatic "yes." A complex mix of guilt and relief ensued. The more she took measures to protect herself, the guiltier she felt and yet the greater the relief that suffused her dealings with others.

After more than a year of such questioning and observation, she noted a slow shift taking place in her self-image. She still winced at her tendency to deny her own needs, but she had much more compassion for herself. "It's such a struggle. The roots of this run incredibly deep in me. I am so eager to sacrifice myself, it's embarrassing. I still want to do it, even though it's great when I manage to hold back. It's such a relief not to be operating by what I am expected to be."

Resistance from loved ones is a particularly wrenching aspect of such transformation. When we make a shift of this magnitude, others' expectations often make it hard to stay the course. Friends and family members may pressure us to keep things the same, especially if nagging doubts about their own path in life have been evoked and they are not ready to address what is coming up for them. They may assail us with reasons to keep within the limits of the known, as they watch change occurring in such close proximity to their stasis.

She continued to serve as a source of succor for those who counted on her, but with a new watchfulness. When a family member called on her, she made herself pause to weigh how much of an interruption from her own affairs was truly warranted. When she faced protest or complaint about these new limits, she repeated to herself that she would be of no use to anyone if she wore herself out. At work, she learned how to postpone rescuing colleagues when her own deadlines put a knot in her stomach. Her determination remained intact, even as she acted in ways that would have been unthinkable for her in the past.

Our weaknesses and strengths are often intertwined. Contending squarely with our vulnerability may also mean affirming the source of our vigor and sensitivity. She finally accepted that her capacity for helpfulness and generosity needed to be balanced with at least some degree of self-protection, and this recognition led to a more durable self-respect.

The prospect of remaking ourselves in later life can be unnerving even as it is exciting, while the lure of safety is relentless. Reasons for deferral are always both plentiful and sensible. Practical considerations can easily convince us that it would be better to wait for a more opportune time to make changes. Relaxing into mindlessness is so much easier than engaging the heart.

At fifty-eight, a woman had her third recurrence of breast cancer. Full of fear and weary of working twelve hours a day as an auditor for a top-notch firm, she consulted her older brother. He invited her to spend a few weeks with his family at their beach-front condo in Mexico. At first she declined, claiming her partners would be furious with her and important contracts delayed if she vanished for such an extended period. Her brother pestered her, calling often and leaving messages that finally goaded her into taking the time off.

Lying on the beach together, their feet extending close to the water's edge, he asked her what would be the most meaningful way she could spend the rest of her life. The surf was spraying their legs with each surge from the powerful swells. Seagulls were squawking. He had waited a full week to spur this dialogue, hoping to pin her down once she had shed the tensions of her job. The question itself was like the challenge of the sea, beyond time and petty concerns.

At first, she did not know how to reply. He took her back to their younger days, before they owned houses and were encumbered with responsibilities. He pressed her to think of parts of herself she had never developed but which had tugged at her long ago. That night, she had a dream in which she was teaching a class of enraptured students. The next morning at breakfast, she recounted the dream and her old hope of becoming a teacher that had gotten suppressed in her desire for financial security.

She returned to her busy life, but the memory of that beach conversation worked on her. Several months later she quit her job, sold her house, and moved to another state where she got a job as a low-paid adjunct faculty member at a university. She was surprised at how quickly she took to teaching, finding that she could animate a classroom with as much alacrity as the finest teachers she had known. A year into her new life, she told her brother that she had never been happier and that she was now ready if it was her time to die, because she had finally gotten to fulfill her longing.

A businessman in his mid-fifties realized he was bored by his own enterprises, lucrative though they had been for years. While on a vacation in Central America, he met some indigenous entrepreneurs. He saw that they needed guidance in how to eliminate the middleman and sell their wares directly on the world market. He went back home, cashed out of his former endeavors, and began coaching these budding third-world businesses. Whole villages began raising their standard of living. "I always wanted to make a difference, to do something about the suffering in the world. All along, while I was earning a living, raising my children, doing conventional things, this need to do more with my life only got stronger." He spoke with an expansive and vibrant tone that flowed directly from having followed his heart's desire.

With time's constriction pressing on us, breaking out of the tried-and-true becomes necessary. We declare that the slumber of deferral is over and that it is time to live in accordance with all that is in us. We are ready to release the energy of our dormant inclinations and be true to ourselves. We vow to exchange that which has been serviceable in our lives for that which could be vivacious. These realms are open to each of us as soon as we are ready to accede to our finest audacity.

24
WHAT MATTERS MOST

Teach us to number our days, that we
may get us a heart of wisdom.

PSALM 90:12

In her old age, the writer Doris Lessing attests to "a fresh liveliness in experiencing . . . as if some gauze or screen has been dissolved away from life that was dulling it." She continues:

You are taken, shaken, by moments when the improbability of our lives comes over you like a fever. Everything is remarkable, people, living, events present themselves to you with the immediacy of players in some barbarous and splendid drama that it seems we are a part of. You have been given new eyes. This must be what a very small child feels, looking out at the world for the first time: everything a wonder.[1]

Anything that makes death real — an illness, the loss of someone beloved — convinces us to clear a space in our lives for what really matters. The energy of finitude impels us to speak what is true for us and to act on our deepest purposes. More ardently than ever, we reach into the soul's domain. We seize upon the great and the small, the lofty and the sensate, with the immediacy demanded by our transience.

Laura Carstensen, a Stanford professor who studies aging, claims that older people are better at living in the present, at focusing on immediate feelings rather than long-term goals. She observes, "When young people look at older people, they think how terrifying it must be to be nearing the end of your life. But older people know what matters most."[2] A woman verging on her one-hundred-and-second birthday told me, "When I wake up in the middle of the night, I'm so glad. It's extra time to think. It's only fifteen minutes or so, then I go back to sleep." Each morning, she marvels that she is still here and wonders what the day will bring.

On a mid-August afternoon, I encountered an 83-year-old woman in a blueberry patch. Her daughter, who was off picking berries in another row, had taken her there as an outing, to get away from the adult-care home into which she had recently moved. Both had always relished being out in the beauty of the world together. I asked if she missed her former residence, an assisted-living facility where she had made many friends and retained some independence. "At my age, you don't get as attached. You move from one life stage to another. It doesn't matter where you are. You take things easier." She laughed as I held her bowl of berries and insisted on helping her across the lumpy grass with her walker, one careful step at a time. "It wouldn't be so bad to take a tumble here," she assured me.

Risk is an essential aspect of aliveness, just as growth often results from loss, and change is almost always accompanied by fear. As we get older, we become well acquainted with loss, but the key is to go on risking and changing despite the fear. We must let it all call us to a finer attention. I grasped her arm as we proceeded, speechless in admiration for her refusal to accept limits to joy.

Many of our constraints take on fresh pointlessness — ceaselessly taking care of tasks, wasting time with people we do not enjoy, ruminating over tomorrow's worries. We become determined to do only that

which is truly necessary or definitely delight-
ful. Aging itself grants us a bolder spirit,
demanding as it does our flexibility and
rewarding us with the freedom to take a
tumble, with the abandon of lying splayed
across the grass.

The most resonant interludes in life occur
when we enter into unfamiliar territory, letting risk shake us up and bestow appreciation. A 58-year-old woman decided to
become a hospice volunteer on the weekends, in order to confront her deepest dread
head-on:

I had been on a certain path for many
years. I had a kind of superstructure I lived
within, which was quite secure. It served
me well for a long time, but then it wasn't
working for me. More and more, I was
wondering what it meant to be ready to
die. A fear of death had been creeping up
on me as I got older. I figured dying people
could show me the territory. It's been an
education, way beyond anything I'd hoped
for, and yet it's only been a little more than
a year. I am now living how I want to die.
There's no other way to put it. I'm not
afraid anymore.

On the other side of fear is a generative

sense that anything can happen, that we can dare to probe yet another corner of experience. An adventurous attitude gives us reasons to stay alert, especially if retirement has afflicted us with too much sameness, or bereavement has weighed down our spirit. At seventy-three, Eric De Deyner took up the sport of hang gliding: "I happen to be into hang gliding because I get a thrill out of the experience. . . . It's the nearest thing to being a bird." Eleanor Hyndman took up karate at the age of seventy-eight, going to training sessions along with her grandson. She found it gave her "mental sharpness and self-confidence."[3] Frank Levine did not start running until he was sixty-five and his wife was in a nursing home. A friend suggested the idea of running together. When he turned ninety-five, he got to be the youngest in the 95-to-99 bracket in the track-and-field masters competitions. "It makes you look forward to getting older," he remarked.[4]

When life's end seems near, a lifetime of rushing around and striving toward the next goal may subside into appreciation for what is right in front of us. If we let it, scarcity of time ahead breeds attentiveness. We can decide to take life much easier and accept the immediate arena in which pleasure is located. Instead of feeling oppressed by our sense of time running out, we reclaim the art of being. We become energized by celebrating the blink of time we get to be alive. We may find there is time for everything.

A friend nearing retirement was working harder than ever, trying to save up money so that he would have enough when he finally left his job. I asked him where in his extensive yard he best liked to sit on a beautiful summer day. He looked at me, stricken, and said, "I haven't sat out there in years." He realized that he had been filling all of his spare time with projects from work he had taken home with him. The next morning, he got up early and sat outside to listen to birdsong before he started his workday. He had decided there was time for this, and so there was.

The body's lessons are chiefly about savoring. Our aching joints become a metronome ticking out the passage of the days. As we become more aware of abilities that can go at any moment, we tend to take less for granted about even our most ordinary powers. Vibrancy arises from directing our focus to the freedoms we can still seize and the sensory pleasures we can still relish. The soul must push back with increasing vigor each time there is another physical decline. The more losses tug us toward negativity, the more ardently we must bolster our gladness for each capacity that persists.

A 96-year-old woman in assisted living always turned down the safe and predictable van trips provided by her residence. She preferred venturing out by foot on her own, despite her almost total blindness. She liked to push her walker to a nearby center-city park and sit on a bench within the midday commotion. Overhearing the racy lunchtime conversations of women released from their offices was ample entertainment. Sometimes she listened to both crows and homeless people scavenging for their survival in the waste bins not far from her bench. The crows worked quietly and the people made commentary, sometimes blasphemous. After absorbing herself in the spectacle for an hour or so, she would return to her residence revitalized.

To see life as a whole may be the ultimate capacity. As we get older, the context for each painful event widens to the duration of our lifespan. The longer we have lived, the faster we recognize and dispense with the trivial. This broadened perspective causes most of our troubles to shrink and grants an ever-expanding source of solace. It does not offer steady serenity, but rather an increasing ability to rebound from the mishaps that keep coming.

At last, we are convinced that no one is actually better than anyone else and that all along there was nothing to prove. We are ready to live our own truth. Instead of constantly comparing where we stand relative to others, we finally accept ourselves and the life we have lived. We relinquish the project of trying to accomplish something really big. All we want is to exercise our individual gifts and pleasures in peace.

An artist in his early fifties described how he would always panic in the months prior to a show when he was younger. "I still have self-doubts at times about my work, but now I know how to move through it. I gather up my materials and create the right conditions. Discipline to me is clearing out the distractions. I've learned to trust my creativity." Naming and valuing a capacity further enhances it. Over the years, as we identify the ways we sabotage ourselves, we also devise methods for doing our best work. We gradually become emboldened by the intrinsic reward of knowing our capacities will meet the challenges we take on.

At eighty-nine, Carmen Herrera sold her

first painting. After a lifetime of working in obscurity, she attained the age of ninety-four to find her paintings were in demand. Asked about having persevered for so long with little external affirmation, she explained: "I do it because I have to do it; it's a compulsion that also gives me pleasure. I never in my life had any idea of money and I thought fame was a very vulgar thing. So I just worked and waited. And at the end of my life, I'm getting a lot of recognition, to my amazement and my pleasure, actually."[5]

Over the course of a lifetime, living in accordance with our true nature becomes increasingly vital to us. We reach later life ready to live without apology, having developed our own gauges of progress. Acclaim for our efforts is satisfying, should it arise, but it is not the gauge of having lived a worthy life.

After years of struggling with assertion and accomplishment, we come to see that there is not one right way to live. We no longer need to try to bend situations to conform to our particular vision of how things should turn out. A 63-year-old man explained, "I don't have to fix things anymore. I used to put in lots of effort trying to make things proceed as I saw fit, or I'd barrel my way through. Now I figure out ways to work around problems I run into, and that's good enough for me."

Eventually, we stop trying to hold on to the reins. Control was never real to begin with, but in later life we have less need for this illusion. We become less directive, finally acceding to our narrow sphere of influence and the vast unknowable accidents of daily life. We recognize how many of our prior doubts have proven misplaced and that no one gets to implement the fine print of their hopes. Since most things have not worked out as we expected, we understand how futile it was to have worried so much. We realize that grand purposes have been overrated and what matters in the long run is the quality of our individual days.

A friend's 81-year-old mother grieved hard after her husband of sixty years died. She had already lost many of her old friends. After a year of mourning, she sold their old house and moved to a community on the edge of the desert in Arizona. Early every morning, she went out walking on a trail through sagebrush and cacti with a group of six, her neighborhood walking buddies. She was more than thirty years older than the next oldest in her gang, and yet no one seemed to notice. A few years later, I sat with her in the hospital when she came to

Seattle to die. She was an entirely different person than the woman I had known over the years. Rising out of that deep grief had cleansed her of pettiness. She was open to other people's interests and experiences like never before. Even through the ravages of her last illness, she exuded animation from those vivid mornings in the desert with her friends.

I once stepped outside the hospital for a break from a bedside vigil for a friend who was dying. I was startled by the splendor of the afternoon. People were going about the business of living, bustling around, oblivious to approaching death. I walked with the acute sensitivity of sorrow, reveling in the gleam of the sunlight on the sidewalk and the sensation of my full, healthy stride. Loss becomes the great elixir.

The challenge is to keep such clarity once sorrow abates. This happens more readily for me these days, in my fifties, and will keep becoming more prominent. When I was younger, I lapsed more easily into inattention and living with the dull confidence that my capacities and my beloved ones would still be there tomorrow. Now I suffer less unawareness.

I was recently in the presence of someone

dying at the age of sixty-nine. Six days before her death, she did not care about most of the things to which we attach so much importance. She had put her burdens down. There was bemusement in her expression toward her visitors, for what we were all still holding. She was the embodiment of gratitude — for having time yet to say her goodbyes, for the outpouring of support she was receiving from her community. Her gaze is still with me. I want to keep it in my mind's eye.

The literary critic Anatole Broyard was told at sixty-nine that he had prostate cancer that had already spread to his lymph nodes. He wrote:

The knowledge that you're ill is one of the momentous experiences in life. You expect that you're going to go on forever, that you're immortal. Freud said that every man is convinced of his own immortality. I certainly was. I had dawdled through life up to that point, and when the doctor told me I was ill it was like an immense electric shock. I felt galvanized. I was a new person. All of my old trivial selves fell away, and I was reduced to essence.[6]

With death in sight, all that we had previously kept in the background as we went about the business of living is called to the foreground of our attention. We look back at our prior mishaps and victories, all that has burdened and pleased us, and perceive what has happened in a different way. Things that need to be spoken can get said, gratitude can be conveyed, apologies can be rendered, and feelings hidden at the price of long loneliness can be risked. With the consciousness that time is running out, we tend to make sure others know how well they are loved.

In her late fifties, a friend of mine started bringing death into every conversation. She made people nervous. Frequently, her sentences began with the phrase, "When I die . . ." and took off from there. This phrase prompted those in her vicinity to glimpse their own demise. Some fled her company. But by summoning this consciousness, my friend called for enthusiasm rather than anxiety, vivaciousness rather than a dirge.

A woman in her forties who lost her mother in her early twenties claimed that vivid images from her mother's last days still accompanied her in her daily life. "I picture my mother — skin and bones — enraged about having to leave life before fifty. She still had so much she wanted to do. So I get things done. I say what I want to say, and nobody gets away with wasting my time." This woman was old before her time, in all of the best ways.

At the age of fifty-five, I was snorkeling at the Great Barrier Reef off the northeast coast of Australia, trying to take in the beauty of the spectacle below me — the bright colors of the coral, the sleek movement of the fish, and the splendor of living things for whom human life is entirely irrelevant. I had only a half hour ahead of me before the call would come to get back into the boat for the return trip to land, and I knew I was unlikely to come back to this spot ever again.

I wanted to hold on to what I was experiencing, to clutch it to me and not let go. Then it occurred to me that the only thing to do was to open myself fully to what was in front of me. I was putting all of it into the basket of memory, to be taken out later and savored. I saw that it was best to meld myself into the scene without more urgency than any of the fish swimming by.

A 96-year-old man announced that he had fallen in love. He told me he was waking up in the morning and singing. He was thinking of his beloved all the time, counting the hours until they were reunited. Each evening, they would listen to opera and have some of the best conversations of their lives. He felt lighthearted and wonderfully foolish. "Who would have thought this would have happened to me?"

Memento mori — remember we must die. When life is lived this way, we avert our eyes from petty concerns and focus on what is most important. We are far better able to bear what befalls us. We do not miss a chance to sit on the porch and listen to birdsong in the morning, or pay attention to a loved one and prize our time together. The answer to death is to live more heartily.

Near the conclusion of Ingmar Bergman's film *Fanny and Alexander,* the patriarch at a family banquet stands up and makes a speech to the young faces arrayed down both sides of the table. He ends with an admonition about how to live: "Therefore let us be happy while we are happy, let us be kind, generous, affectionate, and good. Therefore it is necessary, and not in the least shameful, to take pleasure in the little world, good food, gentle smiles, fruit trees in bloom, waltzes."[7]

While visiting my father's grave a few years ago, I glanced over at the adjacent patch of ground I had reserved for myself and my husband. It was a sunny morning in early spring, with fresh grass coming up and new leaves opening in the trees. I examined the earth that will be upturned someday to receive my casket, seeing a quick vision of the mourners who will gather here for me. Then I shook off the image and felt defiantly alive, animated by the privilege of not yet being dead. I had the distinct joy of a day ahead of me waiting to be lived.

EPILOGUE

When I chose a graduate school concentration on aging, I did not suspect that being around elders for the next thirty years would so completely change the way I lived. I was twenty-six years old. I thought elders were over there somewhere, in a quadrant apart from me, to be studied or helped or managed. Instead, I got drawn into a great continuous flow which included me and them, and eventually all the ages in them and myself.

I became old when I was young. I found out that *old* can be a wonderful state of being, more than a condition of the body. Just as older people feel their youth inside them, I began to feel — and celebrate — the *old lady* in myself. I became more aware of frailty and death, and therefore also the glory of being able to see, hear, smell, walk, and live. I put my heart into friendships that were fully reciprocal and likely to last. I sought and found a life partner with whom interesting conversation would not run out and who would put a high value on building something worth keeping. I have not been afraid of growing old, because I have been conscious of growing. The more I know about life, the better I am at living. I wish this awareness for everyone.

The film that says it best is *Ikiru* (*To Live*) by Akira Kurosawa. A career bureaucrat learns he has terminal cancer and finds he can no longer stand to handle the piles of papers on his desk as he has done five days a week for more than forty years. Setting out to redeem his life, he searches for something he can do for his community. In the final scene, he is sitting on a swing in the inner-city playground he helped build, smiling in the face of death. The snow is falling, and his eyes are radiant.

NOTES

INTRODUCTION

1. Katherine Askew, "Emotional Component of Wisdom," blog response (June 3, 2010), www.ChangingAging.org.
2. Arthur A. Stone, Joseph E. Schwartz, Joan E. Broderick, and Angus Deaton, "A Snapshot of the Age Distribution of Psychological Well-Being in the United States," *Proceedings of the National Academy of Sciences of the United States of America* (PNAS) 107, no. 22 (May 2010).

CHAPTER 1. SELF-KNOWLEDGE

1. Nancy Wick, "From Academic to Artist: Richey Retires to New Career," University [of Washington] Weekly online newsletter, October 30, 2008.

CHAPTER 3. THE GREAT LEVELING

1. Interview by Marcy Stamper, *Methow Valley News,* January 28, 2009.

2. Harry R. Moody and David Carroll, *The Five Stages of the Soul* (New York: Anchor Books/Doubleday, 1997), 98–99.

Chapter 4. Relationships

1. Susanne Scheibe and Laura L. Carstensen, "Emotional Aging: Recent Findings and Future Trends," *Journal of Gerontology* 65B, no. 2 (March 2010).
2. Susan Scarf Merrel, *The Accidental Bond: The Power of Sibling Relationships* (New York: Times Books, 1995), 219.
3. Connie Goldman, *Late-Life Love: Romance and New Relationships in Later Years* (Minneapolis: Fairview Press, 2006), 145.

Chapter 5. Loss

1. Interview by Scott Simon, *Weekend Edition,* National Public Radio, December 18, 2009.
2. Jay Allison and Dan Gediman, eds., *This I Believe* (New York: Henry Holt, 2006), 14.

Chapter 6. Spirituality

1. Interview by Stewart Kampel, *Hadassah Magazine,* August/September 2009.
2. Arthur Frank, *At the Will of the Body:*

Reflections on Illness (Boston: Houghton Mifflin, 1991), 142.

3. Peter Fimrite, "Daring Rescue of Whale off Farallones," *San Francisco Chronicle,* December 14, 2005, A-1.

4. *High Holiday Prayer Book,* p. 345.

5. Excerpt from the film *In Her Own Time,* posted at Jewish Women's Archive, http://jwa.org/historymakers/myerhoff/finding-rituals.

CHAPTER 7. GENEROSITY

1. Mery Galanternick, obituary, *The New York Times,* November 11, 2009.

2. Diana Athill, *Somewhere Towards the End: A Memoir* (New York: Norton, 2008), 84.

3. Erik H. Erikson, *Childhood and Society* (New York: Norton, 1950).

CHAPTER 8. GIVING AND RECEIVING

1. Beth Witrogen McLeod, *Caregiving: The Spiritual Journey of Love, Loss, and Renewal* (New York: Wiley, 1999), 66–67.

2. Capitol Hill Village, www.capitolhillvillage.org.

3. Barbara Myerhoff, *Number Our Days* (New York: Simon & Schuster, 1978).

4. Beth Howard, "The Secrets of Resilient People," *AARP Magazine,* November/

December 2009, 37.

Chapter 9. Time

1. John Bleibtreu, *The Parable of the Beast* (New York: Macmillan, 1968), 3–4.
2. Kenneth R. Lakritz and Thomas M. Knoblauch, *Elders on Love: Dialogues on the Consciousness, Cultivation, and Expression of Love* (New York: Parabola Books, 1999), 176.
3. Sara Lawrence-Lightfoot, *The Third Chapter: Passion, Risk, and Adventure in the 25 Years after 50* (New York: Farrar, Straus and Giroux, 2009), 139.

Chapter 10. Hindsight

1. Interview by Dave Beck, "A Father's Musical Discouragement," *Sound Focus,* KUOW (Seattle), February 11, 2009.

Chapter 11. Decisions

1. Frances Moore Lappé and Jeffrey Perkins, *You Have the Power: Choosing Courage in a Culture of Fear* (New York: Tarcher/Penguin, 2005), 44–45.

Chapter 12. Detours

1. Caroline Knapp, *Drinking: A Love Story* (New York: Dell, 1996).
2. Interview by Jacki Lyden, *Weekend Edi-*

tion, National Public Radio, December 20, 2009.
3. Interview by Nancy Griffin, *AARP Magazine,* May/June 2008.

CHAPTER 13. RESILIENCE

1. Gene D. Cohen, "The New Senior Moment," *Aging Well,* Winter 2008, 50.
2. http://oldathlete.blogspot.com/2009/11/mental-edge.html, "Snappy."
3. Joshua Wolf Shenk, "What Makes Us Happy?" *The Atlantic,* June 2009.

CHAPTER 14. COHERENCE

1. Ronald Manheimer, *A Map to the End of Time: Wayfarings with Friends and Philosophers* (New York: Norton, 1999), 24–25.

CHAPTER 15. STORIES

1. Carter Catlett Williams, *Glorious Adventure* (New York: Pioneer Network for Culture Change, 2008).

CHAPTER 17. COURAGE

1. Brendan Gill, *Late Bloomers* (New York: Workman, 1996), 72.
2. Steve Perry, "Grumpy Old Archetypes" (September 10, 1999), http://www.salon.com/books/int/1999/09/10/hillman.

CHAPTER 18. THE BODY'S LESSONS

1. Interview by Marcie Sillman, *Old Masters,* KUOW (Seattle), April 10, 2009.
2. Ada C. Perry, "One Hundred Gifts," in *Gifts of Age: Portraits and Essays of 32 Remarkable Women,* eds. Charlotte Painter and Pamela Valois (San Francisco: Chronicle Books, 1985), 124.
3. Susan Jacoby, "Real Life Among the Old Old," *The New York Times,* December 30, 2010, A-23.

CHAPTER 19. ATTITUDE

1. "Mind Over Matter," a conversation between Stanley Kunitz and his assistant, Genine Lentine, *Poetry Foundation* (October 4, 2006), www.poetryfoundation.org/journal/article.html?id=178263.
2. Robert L. Weber, "Searching for the Curative Power of Gratitude and Forgiveness in Groups," *The Group Circle: The Newsletter of the American Group Psychotherapy Association* 1:6 (Fall 2005).
3. Henri J. M. Nouwen and Walter J. Gaffney, *Aging: The Fulfillment of Life* (New York: Imago Books/Doubleday, 1990), 76–77.

CHAPTER 20. SLOWING DOWN

1. Jan Fawcett, M.D., "Aging Seems Nonlinear," *Psychiatric Annals* 39 (September 2009), 824.
2. Rona Spalten, "The Jewel," in *Filtered Images: Women Remembering Their Grandmothers,* ed. Susan L. Aglietti (Orinda, CA: Vintage '45 Press, 1992), 161.

CHAPTER 21. COMPOSURE

1. Neenah Ellis, *If I Live to be 100: Lessons from the Centenarians* (New York: Crown, 2002), 42.

CHAPTER 22. BEGINNER'S MIND

1. C. G. Jung, *Memories, Dreams, Reflections* (New York: Vintage Books, 1963), 358.

CHAPTER 24. WHAT MATTERS MOST

1. John Burningham, *The Time of Your Life: Getting On with Getting On* (London: Bloomsbury, 2002), 271.
2. "The U-Bend of Life: Why, Beyond Middle Age, People Get Happier as They Get Older," *Economist,* December 18, 2010, 36.
3. Etta Clark, "Late Bloomers: Growing Old is not for Sissies. Portraits of Senior

Athletes," *American Fitness,* November/ December 1991.

4. John Leland, "Elderly Athletes," *The New York Times,* August 19, 2009.

5. Deborah Sontag, "At 94, She's the Hot New Thing in Painting," *The New York Times,* December 20, 2009.

6. Anatole Broyard, *Intoxicated by My Illness and Other Writings on Life and Death* (New York: Ballantine, 1992), 37–38.

7. Ingmar Bergman, *Fanny and Alexander,* Alan Blair, trans. (New York: Pantheon Books, 1982), 208.

ABOUT THE AUTHOR

Wendy Lustbader, MSW, is an author, social worker, and professor who works with older people, and their families and caregivers, and lectures nationally on subjects related to aging. She is the author of *Taking Care of Aging Family Members* (coauthored with Nancy R. Hooyman), *Counting on Kindness,* and *What's Worth Knowing.* She lives in Seattle with her husband, Barry Grosskopf, an author and psychiatrist.